"If having a systematic game plan for obtaining a job appeals to you, you will love *Fearless Job Hunting*. The authors provide very practical information for every step of the job-hunting process. Most importantly, with the power of cognitive behavioral therapy, *Fearless Job Hunting* will teach you how to think rationally so that you can get out of your own way to get the job of your dreams."

> —Aldo R. Pucci, Psy.D., president of the National Association
> of Cognitive-Behavioral Therapists

"Anxiety and hopelessness about the ravages of unwanted unemployment have paralyzed countless millions of Americans. Many desperately seek advice on how to restart or change their careers. Through sound and powerful scientifically tested principles, compassion, and reader-friendly exercises, *Fearless Job Hunting* will become the new standard handbook for finding the right job at the earliest time."

> —Barry Lubetkin, Ph.D., founding copresident of the
> Behavioral Therapy Center in New York

"If you are seeking work, thinking of changing jobs, or know people struggling with unemployment, then this is a must-read book for you. *Fearless Job Hunting* goes far beyond the how-to, cookie-cutter books found in this field. I highly recommend this book to anyone who wants to get employed sooner rather than later."

> —Richard S. Schneiman, Ph.D., codirector of the
> Intermountain Center for REBT in Salt Lake City, UT.

"This is a timely book for those whom the global financial crisis has thrown out of work and young people entering the job market for the first time. This hands-on manual shows you how to present your strengths and capabilities in a competitive job-seeking market. It demonstrates how to reduce negative thinking—for example, thoughts of low self-worth—and how to manage anxiety-provoking interviews. The book contains many useful check lists, tables, and two valuable chapters on communication skills and résumé preparation. I recommend it to job seekers both young and old seeking to optimize their chances of getting the jobs they want."

> —Antony Kidman, AM, Ph.D., director of the Health Psychology Unit at the University of Technology in Sydney, Australia

"Learn to use powerful psychological principles to create an efficient job-search environment, network, communicate effectively with employers, and keep moving forward when the going gets tough. Whether you are looking for a dream job or just one to get by with for now, use this complete job search reference to give yourself a winning edge and get the job you want."

> —Janet Wolfe, Ph.D., former executive director of the Albert Ellis Institute and adjunct professor at New York University

"A sane and practical book on getting the job you want. Don't put this book down—run to the check-out counter. Then use the book to help yourself land that great job."

> —Vincent E. Parr, Ph.D., president of the Rational Living Foundation

FEARLESS
JOB
HUNTING

POWERFUL PSYCHOLOGICAL
STRATEGIES FOR
GETTING THE JOB YOU WANT

BILL KNAUS, ED.D.
SAM KLARREICH, PH.D.
RUSSELL GRIEGER, PH.D.
NANCY KNAUS, MBA, PH.D.

NEW HARBINGER PUBLICATIONS, INC.

Publisher's Note

This publication is designed to provide accurate and authoritative information in regard to the subject matter covered. It is sold with the understanding that the publisher is not engaged in rendering psychological, financial, legal, or other professional services. If expert assistance or counseling is needed, the services of a competent professional should be sought.

Distributed in Canada by Raincoast Books

Copyright © 2010 by Bill Knaus, Ed.D., Sam Klarreich, Ph.D., Russell Grieger, Ph.D., Nancy Knaus, MBA, Ph.D.
New Harbinger Publications, Inc.
5674 Shattuck Avenue
Oakland, CA 94609
www.newharbinger.com

All Rights Reserved
Printed in the United States of America

Acquired by Jess O'Brien; Cover design by Amy Shoup;
Edited by Nelda Street; Text design by Tracy Marie Carlson

FSC
Mixed Sources
Product group from well-managed forests and other controlled sources

Cert no. SW-COC-002283
www.fsc.org
© 1996 Forest Stewardship Council

Library of Congress Cataloging-in-Publication Data

Fearless job hunting : powerful psychological strategies for getting the job you want / Bill Knaus ... [et al.] ; foreword by George S. Elias.
   p. cm.
Includes bibliographical references.
ISBN 978-1-57224-834-2
1. Job hunting. I. Knaus, William J.
HF5382.7.F43 2010
650.14--dc22

                              2010009351

12 11 10   10 9 8 7 6 5 4 3 2 1   First printing

CONTENTS

PART 1

GEAR UP TO MANAGE YOUR JOB-LOSS AND JOB-SEARCH CHALLENGES

PART 2

GET ROLLING ON A SUCCESSFUL JOB SEARCH

PART 3

CLOSE THE DEAL BY CONTACTING DECISION MAKERS, PRESENTING EFFECTIVELY, AND NEGOTIATING YOUR CONTRACT

FOREWORD

When was the last time you made a decision? In all probability, it was moments ago. Making decisions is an inescapable necessity. Were you consciously aware of having made a decision—and, if so, were you aware of the process you used? Decision making is one-third logical and two-thirds psychological.

As adults, we have been formed by the many influences in our environment. These include experiences in which we have actively participated, such as formal education, supervised job training, and employment. Other influences arose outside our control, yet they exerted an equal—if not stronger—role in our development. Collectively, these influences give direction to how we make decisions.

The requirements for making a decision are deceptively simple: knowledge of the past, present knowledge, and awareness of future possibilities. In order to arrive at a decision, you must first consider those factors in the past that are relevant to the pending decision. Next, you will want to consider conditions that exist at the moment. Before making your final decision, you must give careful thought to what the results of your choice might be.

Reviewing the three requirements, it would appear that decision making is a relatively easy process to execute. Its simplicity should allow you not only to make a decision, but to make the decision that is the most appropriate. Yet, we know that this is not always true.

Relevant and accurate information is essential. In job hunting, two major sources of information serve as a basis for decision making: knowledge of the world of work in which you will function, and self-knowledge. Knowing yourself is the key that opens the door through which you will travel on your journey to fearless job hunting. Nonetheless, to know yourself is both necessary and potentially threatening. The process is fertile ground for the seeds of procrastination.

However sufficient the information appears to be, and however well we attend to the three requirements of decision making, it's still difficult to be sure that we are making the best decision. This book will help. *Fearless Job Hunting* addresses both the one-third that is logical and the two-thirds that is psychological. To achieve your goal requires effort; however, it will be well worth it.

You are about to start an interesting and exciting trip. Bon voyage!

—George S. Elias, Ed.D.

ACKNOWLEDGMENTS

We wish to acknowledge the following business professionals, who provided useful comments for this book: John Hazen, president of Hazen Paper Company; William Wagner, president of Chicopee Savings Bank; Michael Stacey, manager of human resources at Tyco Fire and Security (retired); Diane B. Nadeau, president of Action Business Services; Rina Cohen, attorney at law; Robert Forester, vice president of marketing, New England Etching Company (retired); Arthur Mason, automotive service manager (retired); and John Gallup, president of Strathmore Paper Company (retired).

INTRODUCTION

Fearless Job Hunting is for you if you want to:

➤ Rebound from a job loss by taking quick and effective action to find a better job

➤ Work for a different company to advance your career interests

➤ Move from part-time to full-time work

➤ Change your career direction

➤ Add to your retirement income

➤ Obtain a great entry-level job

Going way beyond traditional job-search books, *Fearless Job Hunting* teaches you how to overcome psychological obstacles, conduct a successful job search, impress decision makers, and close the deal. We'll show you how to shift your job search into high gear with a little muscle and some powerful practical strategies. And because knowing yourself, including your strengths and limitations, is important for getting on a strong career track, we'll show you how to match your interests and abilities to your ideal job. You'll learn how to get through to the "gatekeepers," the people who can pave your way to an interview—and a great job. You'll find tips based on scientifically tested psychological methods and communication skills development methods to help you communicate effectively with interviewers and give knowledgeable responses. The psychological methods include applying evidence-based rational emotive behavior therapy (REBT) and cognitive behavioral therapy (CBT) to promote positive and realistic job-search thoughts, emotional strength, and effective search actions. Arming yourself with this valuable information can boost your confidence and help erase the stress, uncertainty, and procrastination that can obstruct a timely and successful search.

In a long-term study focused on job-search persistence and intensity (how hard one looks for work), two factors were key to a more effective job search and, ultimately, getting a job: (1) having a positive self-evaluation and (2) being prepared, which included following through with plans (Wanberg et al. 2005). You'll learn ways to persist by applying proven job-search strategies (ibid.).

Nineteenth-century military strategist Carl von Clausewitz (1968 [1832]) emphasized the importance of preparation in any strategic campaign. Preparation strongly influences the outcome of the decisions you make and actions you take. Flexibly persisting with your job-search strategies and methods sharpens the trajectory of your search. To support this awareness and action approach to successfully conducting your job search, we've divided this book into three tactical sections. You'll learn how to:

> ➤ *Gear up to manage your job-loss and job-search challenges* by reducing your stress, following through effectively on important tasks, and optimizing your search performance.

> ➤ *Get rolling on a successful job search* by creating a positive work environment for conducting your search; producing a job-hunting profile that represents your strengths, interests, and values; designing a powerful résumé and cover letter; getting job referrals through networking; and using search firms productively.

> ➤ *Close the deal by contacting decision makers, presenting effectively, and negotiating your contract.* You'll learn how to get through to decision makers, communicate effectively, make the most of your interview opportunities, and complete the process by negotiating a great deal.

Each chapter includes quick tips that highlight the chapter's key points; plus, at the end of each chapter is a four-point performance-tracking system for a successful search, comprising:

➤ Key Ideas

➤ Action Steps

➤ Implementation

➤ Results

Use this system to record what you learned from the chapter, to prepare yourself for action, and to execute and modify your actions based on what you learned. If you interact with the chapter information this way, your fearless-job-hunting path will bring you the success you seek. We believe this more personal approach can help you significantly reduce the time it takes to get that great job you want and deserve.

PART 1

Gear Up to Manage Your Job-Loss and Job-Search Challenges

1 PREP YOURSELF FOR POSITIVE ACTION

In *Fearless Job Hunting* we'll serve as your GPS (global positioning system) by pointing you toward strategies, tools, and tips for accelerating your job hunt. You'll learn powerful psychological and business management tactics for taking charge of yourself, getting to the gatekeepers (decision makers), and presenting yourself effectively to land that coveted job.

In traveling this purposeful and productive path, *you* will be the agent of action, using and expanding your capabilities to successfully complete your job search. Along this path, you may find certain consistent obstacles, some of which you unintentionally generate yourself. This chapter will start you on your way to overcoming these consistent errors, including how to recognize them and how to step on a productive path with fewer needless hassles.

Armed with your own job-search GPS, you'll take charge of yourself. In the spirit of unusually productive people, you'll engage in job-search events that are within your means to direct or influence. So put on your seat belt and get ready for an exciting journey!

SIX PEOPLE ON THE HUNT

Although all job searchers face the challenge of getting work and earning pay, you may have unique challenges to meet along the way. Each of the following six example job hunters faces particular challenges. Let us introduce you to fearless job hunters John, Tom, Frank, Sally, Carl, and Mary, each of whom has different motivation and faces different challenges in finding and keeping a great new job.

➤ John

John works for a high-powered advertising firm that prides itself on producing outstanding results and on maintaining excellent customer service—but it's a sweatshop. Like others in the firm, John works eighty or more hours a week—and much more lately, now that the economy is sputtering.

This young manager has a growing family, including a brand-new daughter. Remembering his own dad as an absentee father who was tied to his job, John swore he wouldn't go down that path, but now finds himself following in his father's footsteps. Something has to give. He wants to watch his children's soccer games and to spend more time with his wife, who laughingly says, "Hi, stranger," when he comes home late from the office. Unable to negotiate fewer hours for his current job, John dusts off his résumé and prepares to make a job change.

➤ Tom

Tom felt happy when he stepped onstage to get his college diploma. The world of work beckoned, and he couldn't wait to get started. As an accounting major, he understood the benefits of cutting back on his loan-carrying costs by starting work immediately.

Initially expecting his degree to automatically open doors, Tom winds up finding closed doors. The economy is tanking, as are opportunities in his field. He adjusts his expectations, but after four months of discouragement, Tom is now ready to change his strategy and revitalize his search.

➢ Frank

For the past eight years, Frank has worked in government service, which he originally found challenging. He has been promoted and has received salary increments. Despite having a secure job, over the past several years he has lost interest in his work and he now yearns for a career change. Yet he feels conflicted about taking a risk and worries about making the wrong decision. Realizing he's been getting in his own way, he picks up a copy of Fearless Job Hunting.

➢ Sally

Sally used to run a significant sales department and was renowned for her excellent social skills, persistence, and ability to produce results. Nevertheless, she longed for a family and, once pregnant, decided to be a stay-at-home mom. Three children and twenty years later, Sally is eager to get back to managing a sales force. With many transferable skills, she's open to new options. She knows it's important to retool to restart her career but still feels adrift about where to begin.

➢ Carl

A top performer who deservedly rose to an executive-level position, Carl was one of those rare go-to guys. If you wanted a project done on time and below budget, you let Carl do it. But in a bitter takeover, a rival company assumed control of Carl's company, and heads started to roll. Carl accepted an early retirement package and then busied himself with volunteer work. After a few unexpected financial setbacks and an eagerness to get back to managing projects, this fifty-nine-year-old executive is on the phone networking but finds no red carpet awaiting him. Now Carl has a new project: getting a quality job in a world where age discrimination is a factor he's always known about but never thought would apply to him.

➢ Mary

A small paper company is struggling to maintain its market share and to contain its high labor costs in a declining market—but it's losing the battle. Twenty-five employees are let go, and Mary is one of them. She gets one month of severance and three weeks of vacation pay. Because Mary and her family recently purchased an expensive new home, she and her husband are strapped with a large mortgage. For the next six months, her husband is on tour with the military, and her family counts on her income. She feels stressed to the point where, some days, she just can't get going. Mary's challenge is to put her situation into a less frantic perspective while calmly and persistently taking productive job-search steps.

Each job hunter comes to the search for different reasons and with different strengths and limitations. A knowledgeable, self-disciplined, and patient, yet persistent, approach can tip the balance in your favor. This approach includes knowing yourself and applying your strengths to the challenge of cutting through your personal obstacles and effectively applying the tested job-search strategies in this book.

THE FEARLESS JOB HUNTER

Knowing the psychology involved in a successful search and how to apply it can put you in a catbird seat. The next step is to do what you know. If inertia or procrastination interferes with this process, chapter 3 will show you how to start sweeping these interferences out of the way. Let's start with the fearless job hunter path.

The path of the fearless job hunter is one of productive optimism and enthusiasm. Commitment, determination, and hard work are this path's cobblestones to keep your footing firm. Keeping your eye on the prize (a great new job) will make it easier to translate your job-search goals into effective actions, including setting your goals, sticking to your priorities, planning, researching, communicating effectively, problem solving, negotiating, and closing the deal on your new job.

The fearless path yields a competitive advantage over that of those who buckle from negatives and get bogged down. On the *fearful* path, passivity and procrastination wear you down in your job search, but you'll learn how to shed them as you progress on the *fearless* path.

Resentment over lost opportunities, shame over a lost job, and anxiety about presenting yourself in an interview interfere with your search. These burdens spin from your thoughts concerning your situation and what you think about yourself in the situation. If one thing is in your power to change, it's your self-defeating beliefs. Thinking thoughts that hold you back is a *consistent error* you can correct. Consistent errors are habitual errors that distract you from your job search, such as routinely telling yourself you'll get around to writing your résumé later, which is a typical consistent procrastination error.

CORRECT YOUR CONSISTENT ERRORS IN THINKING

Mistakes happen in any activity, including your job hunt. You might unintentionally forget an appointment, overlook sending out a thank-you note after a successful interview, leave important information out of a cover letter, talk too much or too little during an interview, litter your speech with stock phrases (for example, "like," "you know," and "I mean"), or look away from or stare at your interviewer.

Mistakes, such as spelling errors or forgetting to prepare a follow-up response, are easily correctable once you catch them, and we'll tip you off on how to avoid such errors. But some can easily slide under your awareness. If you tend to downplay your strengths and capabilities due to a misguided sense of humility, this is likely a consistent error. You don't have to go to the opposite extreme to establish a balance, coming across as a braggart—that style may also represent a consistent error. A matter-of-fact presentation in which you emphasize your accomplishments in an informative manner may correct for either extreme.

William James (1842-1910), the father of American psychology, proposed, "The greatest revolution of our generation is the discovery that human beings, by changing the inner attitudes of their minds, can change the outer aspects of their lives." Contemporary evidence supports James's statement (Ellis and Ellis, in press). The implication is clear: you carry your perceptions, beliefs, attitudes, and values with you on your job search, and you can learn to recognize and change the cognitive processes that don't work for you.

If you are like most people, you have blind spots that, of course, are initially hidden from you. For example, if you think the job market is too tight to offer you opportunities, any available jobs will more likely go to those who believe they'll prevail in their search in any job market.

Practically anyone can learn to think realistically and optimistically and stretch farther than ever before. You can learn to recognize and erase consistent errors that interfere with your health, happiness, productivity, and job-search success. Over a thousand articles and studies confirm how irrational beliefs negatively affect emotions and actions, and over four hundred randomly controlled studies show that you can change harmful beliefs, strengthen your realistic beliefs, and motivate yourself to decide and follow through on productive actions.

Consistent errors that cause no harm are rarely more than amusing when discovered. You may believe that grasshoppers can dance to hip-hop beats, but there's absolutely no evidence to support that belief, no more than there's evidence to support the once widely held belief that the world was flat. However, some errors typically get in the way of a fearless job search. These consistent errors come in different forms, such as "if–then," or conditional, thinking, which can distract you from your search. Recognizing the distortion frees you from self-imposed restrictions.

Correct Your If–Then Errors

The *if–then* type of consistent error differs from the problem-solving variety. In the world of the consistent error, the "if" is an assumption and the "then" seems like a fact. Here are three *if–then* pitfalls to avoid, along with some sample antidotes in case you stumble despite your best efforts.

JOB SECURITY: *If the next job I get isn't secure, I'll be making a big mistake. My next job must be secure; otherwise I can't be happy.* This is a showstopper belief, and its antidote is to ponder this question: what job is 100 percent secure? Rather than chase windmills, you'll usually do better by pursuing opportunities that match your skills well and offer opportunities for you to perform effectively.

NEGATIVE FORECASTING: *If I lose my next job, I'll be devastated and ruined forever.* Job hunters who attach their well-being and personal worth to a job set themselves up for unnecessary stress and pain. An antidote is to accept—not like—the fact that job losses are part of work culture, and there's no guarantee of lifelong employment in any company. By shedding this if–then thinking, you realize a job loss is what it is—a loss. Unburdened with if–then thinking, a search is energized and geared toward finding a better job.

ENTITLEMENT THINKING: *If I don't get the job I want, it's not worth the effort.* Fearful job hunters believe they must get what they want in the next job, whether it's guaranteed security, respect, or indispensability. Otherwise, the job's not worth it. That's rarely a realistic way to view a job. The antidote to this form of entitlement thinking is to accept reality. If you catch yourself in this "world revolves around me" trap, you may have forgotten the purpose of a job from the employer's perspective: How can you support the company's mission and goals? What skills do you have to help solve problems? Folks who think this way are more likely to get and keep a job.

But does positive thinking work better than if-then consistent errors? It depends. Using popular ideas about the power of positive thinking, like those of Norman Vincent Peale, where you recite such affirmations as "I'm getting better in every way every day," is a good example of another form of unrealistic thinking. What does this mean on days where disappointments flourish and you make more mistakes than usual? Are you still getting better in every way? You may find that a special form of contingency thinking is embedded in this sophistry: your worth depends on getting better every day. That's a formula for anxiety. Accepting yourself, with all your strengths and limitations, is normally a sound antidote.

Avoid the Looking-Glass Effect

Millions burden themselves with *what if* worries: *What if I don't get a job? What if I make a jerk of myself while interviewing?* This defeatist thinking rarely represents an act of reflective or free inquiry. Usually the answer is automatically built into the question, which is what makes it a consistent error: *I'll fail, and others will think I'm incompetent. I'll make a jerk of myself and never live it down.*

Looking-glass thinking can result in the unreasonable apprehension that not getting a job quickly enough or muffing part of your search will leave you blaming yourself and feeling shamed, embarrassed, or guilt-ridden for being imperfect. This self-inflicted apprehension can lead to *blame-avoidance procrastination*, where you handicap yourself by assuming that your search will end disastrously, so you delay it while awaiting a guarantee of a better outcome. You play it safe by going for jobs that are comfortably beneath your capabilities.

It's rare when any job search flows perfectly. You may be your own worst critic, judging yourself over errors others don't see. If so, this might be a consistent error for you.

The *looking-glass effect*, a common consistent error, is when you think others will judge you for making mistakes. You may see yourself that way, but believing that others think the same way is the looking-glass effect (Cooley 1902).

This consistent error has yet to trickle significantly into public awareness. However, if you catch yourself thinking that others regard you the same as you regard yourself, here's a quick antidote: ask yourself, "Where's the uncontestable evidence that I'll do nothing but defeat myself in my job search?" If you can anticipate how you defeat yourself, you can correct errors at the get-go.

Find the Bottom Line

Consistent errors can appear in subtle ways. Let's look at Carol's situation. She has exceptional talent as a graphic artist—perhaps she's among the very best. She believes she doesn't deserve success, a consistent error that strongly influences her level of aspiration. If Carol has the opportunity to get work that fits her ability, she procrastinates on following through. Such is the power of her negative self-concept that it can rule over her talent and capability. However, a self-concept is built on a foundation of beliefs, and you can change the aspect of your self-concept that includes misguided beliefs.

BOTTOM LINE: Rethink your thinking when you find yourself in a pattern of underselling yourself and consistently landing jobs that are below your capabilities.

Bill gets a nine-month severance package that will continue until he gets a new job. He decides to travel for eight months with his wife and then start his search. In his first interview, the interviewer asks, "What have you done in the past nine months to find work?" Bill discovers a consistent error: he has not identified how an employer will view his work ethic. His perspective on taking time to travel differs from that of most potential employers.

> BOTTOM LINE: In planning a job search, it's wise to take into account what a typical organization looks for in its employees.

Through a family friend, Jill gets an interview for a great job at a regional insurance agency. She buys a new outfit, goes to a hairdresser, does everything in her power to look professional, and, on interview day, spends three hours grooming herself. Initially Jill hits it off with the interviewer until she hears the question, "What do you know about our company?" This becomes the kiss of death, because she knows only where the company is located and that it's an insurance agency. She knows nothing of the organization's history, traditions, and customers.

> BOTTOM LINE: Researching the company is a high priority.

PRESSURE-PROOF YOURSELF

Losing a job presents a hardship for most people. You might assume that anyone who has lost a desired job will feel threatened, but this isn't necessarily so. When your job consistently stresses you out, it simply may not fit you, or the work conditions may be dysfunctional. In this case, you may be delighted to be dismissed or to voluntarily leave for another, more suitable position. A job search is a chance to flip to a new chapter of your life.

In politics, perception is reality. Depending on your situation and your perceptions, you may see a job loss as unbearable, a hardship, an opportunity to explore exciting new options, or something else. Because different people in similar situations can have different views and face different conditions, what's a legitimate choice for one person may not work for another.

The second hand of a clock returns to the same spot every sixty seconds, but time that has passed is in the past. What have you learned that you want to carry forward to your next job? If you left an uncompromising work environment, you are likely to look favorably upon one where decision makers are open to new ideas and willing to compromise for the good of the company. If you view yourself as not fitting into your former employer's concept of a team, look for opportunities to work for a company with a philosophy more compatible with your social interests, perhaps one that has more exciting individuals. If you previously bumped up against a "glass ceiling," look for job openings with advancement opportunities.

Prepare Yourself for Pressure-Proofing

We don't want to sidestep the seriousness of a job loss, the discomfort of remaining in a stressful job, or the challenge of starting a search after being out of the job market. We understand that grieving over a loss is a real and natural reaction. And apprehension about a job search, at any of its phases, is a very normal human reaction. Taking a bad situation and making it worse, however, is discretionary. Amplifying your own stress often represents an automatic but correctable consistent error. For example, if after a job-search setback you declare yourself *destroyed*, you are likely to have a different emotional response than if you viewed the setback as an inconvenience. "Devastated" and "ruined" are words that can amplify stress. They can have a stronger emotional impact than words such as "sad" and "unpleasant."

How you perceive your situation influences how you feel and what you do. If you define your condition as a threat, you'll likely have a different physical reaction than if you viewed the same situation as a challenge. For example, if you view a job hunt as merely a way to survive, you'll likely feel differently than if you believe it will lead to an opportunity to thrive.

You are in control of how you reason things out, or you can at least choose to figure out how to keep challenged by a search and to avoid amplifying your stress. If your thinking makes matters worse, debunk this type of consistent error by obtaining and maintaining a realistic perspective and taking control of your actions.

Refusing to treat emotion-amplifying thoughts as laws brings you fewer negative thoughts, plus the chance to get more of a fix on what you can do to ensure that you find a more productive, profitable, and fulfilling career opportunity.

Pressure-Proof Using Confidence-Boosting Measures

A reality perspective is that of "what is" rather than "what should be." Here are some fearless job hunting options for developing and keeping a realistic perspective.

AMPLIFY ACCEPTANCE. Setbacks, job losses, and job insecurities are facts of life. Fearless job hunters strive to accept the fact that the search process isn't always fair and just. Decision makers may not return calls, may not answer e-mails, may miss appointments, and may select a less capable candidate. Acceptance doesn't mean you have to like it, but an acceptant view frees you from distractions so you can energize and focus on actions that end in a successful search and provide for a sharp beginning.

BOOST YOUR TOLERANCE. If you are afraid of ambiguity and uncertainty, you're not alone. Yet fearless job hunters strive to develop a high tolerance for the unknown. It helps them channel their resources and develop a plan for entering areas of uncertainty to gain clarity and, subsequently, direction. This tolerance buffers you from two inner obstacles that can thwart a quality search: anxiety and procrastination.

USE A CHALLENGE APPROACH. Most people don't look forward to searching for a new job. It takes time and effort, but it also offers opportunity. Fearless job hunters strive to see adverse conditions as opportunities and challenges, rather than threats. A challenge outlook is associated with better coronary functioning (Blascovich 2008), and we've observed that such a view is associated with increased energy, improved output, enhanced self-assurance, and a better chance of getting what you want. For you, a challenge might mean calling a senior executive you've never spoken to before to get information.

If you are interested in more information about pressure-proofing yourself in a work setting, see *Pressure-Proofing: How to Increase Personal Effectiveness on the Job and Anywhere Else for That Matter*, by Sam Klarreich (Routledge, 2008).

Develop Self-Efficacy

Many job hunters feel overwhelmed by the quantity of jobs and the many steps involved in finding a good one. But you can view quantity as a good thing—who doesn't want more options? By learning how to conduct a quality job search and by creating quality support materials, such as a résumé, you position yourself to get a great job from the many available—rather than to just take what you can easily get.

Acting to meet challenges strengthens your coping *self-efficacy*, your belief that you can organize, regulate, and direct your actions to achieve a purposeful result (Bandura 1997). Classic self-efficacy steps include analyzing problems, forming goals, creating road maps to achieve those goals, implementing your plan, evaluating the results, and determining the next course of action. Self-regulating your self-efficacy actions leads to higher-quality performance and less procrastination (Klassen, Krawchuk, and Rajani 2008).

Self-efficacy is a path to mastery and high performance that directly applies to finding a great new job. Indeed, self-efficacy is among the top five psychological contributions of the twentieth and twenty-first centuries and is strongly supported by the scientific literature. While writing this book, we found listed on the American Psychological Association database 16,063 references on self-efficacy that are mainly scientific studies supporting the benefits of self-efficacy beliefs.

Because beliefs can powerfully affect how you feel and what you do, they are a big part of your job-search GPS, and self-efficacy is a great navigating tool to include.

QUICK TIPS

> Decide to pressure-proof yourself.

> Improve your knowledge of yourself by getting to know your strengths and any areas you need to develop and enhance.

> Consider each step of the job hunt as a challenge.

> Identify your skills and competencies; be able to describe them with clarity and use examples and stories to illustrate them.

> Identify and expand any job-hunt strategies that will create meaningful opportunities.

> Seek out companies where you can apply your strongest skills and competencies.

> Pursue organizations where, even if your specific skills aren't suitable, your drive, motivation to learn, and passion can play an important role.

> Hunt for that work environment where you perform at your best and flourish.

PREPARE FOR SUCCESS

To improve your job-search effectiveness, psychologist Connie Wanberg and her colleagues suggest how to persist with higher levels of job-search intensity (Wanberg et al. 2005). We describe and expand on their suggestions as follows:

> People who lost a job tend to experience higher levels of anxiety and a lower sense of worth. It's important to recognize, evaluate, and manage such tendencies.

> Maintain a positive attitude, positive self-view, and accurate self-evaluation by taking a positive, fact-based outlook.

➤ Recognize that you are in control of your search and your progress depends on you; persistence will pay off with a job.

➤ Support your self-efficacy beliefs by taking planned action to achieve your job-search goals.

➤ When feasible, participate in job clubs and support groups with positive-thinking people (avoid contacts with naysayers and people with generally negative attitudes).

➤ Maintain a healthy lifestyle through diet, exercise, and sleep.

➤ Keep to normal daily responsibilities and avoid supporting others' priorities, such as remodeling your basement or watching the dog, which can be a form of procrastination when searching for a job is your priority.

➤ We've observed a tendency in people to slump in their efforts during the job-search process. Resist this temptation.

We find that fearless job hunters show higher self-efficacy and resiliency and get more reward for their search efforts. However, persistence with job-search intensity (how hard you look for work) tends to vary over the span of a search (Kanfer, Wanberg, and Kantrowitz 2001). Being mindful of the inevitability of slumps and making a greater effort than most to work your way past them give you a winning edge. Throughout this book we describe strategies you can use to gain this edge.

The following tracking system is one of many techniques you can use to get up and running and to maintain a reasonable job-search pace.

MONITOR YOUR PROGRESS

A good executive-management technique is to summarize what happened in a meeting or conference immediately afterward and note the next steps. Memory is fallible, so this device not only helps you record where you've been but also shows where you are headed. Now that you have completed this chapter, consider the important points to remember.

A job hunt is an important and pressing activity. Thus, it's a priority and perhaps your top one. Interacting with the material in this book can tip the balance in favor of keeping focused, staying motivated, and actively planning your next steps in the journey to reach your goal of finding and keeping a great job. This part of our GPS-like approach guides you in a solid direction to prepare for and achieve success, based on meeting reasonable objectives.

The first interactive requirement is for you to record "Key Ideas," which are the points that come to mind after you've completed each chapter. In essence this is the "what" you intend to do. Next come the "Action Steps," which are the "how," the way you pursue the key ideas you recorded. Then comes "Implementation," or the "when and who" ideas. Action steps are irrelevant unless you set down specific times you plan to act and the people involved, which is your implementation strategy. Finally come the "Results." After you have carried out your strategy, it's important to examine the results and discover what worked and what didn't, what you might do differently next time, and how you might do it.

Treat the four steps as a nonfailure plan, similar to the approach Thomas Edison took when searching for a durable filament to use in his electric lightbulb. After several thousand different experiments with no solution in sight, he was asked, "How can you take so many failures?" Edison had a quick answer: "I now know what doesn't work."

In working your nonfailure plan, you are testing your plan rather than yourself. Sure, the plan is an extension of what you think, but what you think is not the whole of you. You're a pluralistic person. By approaching a job search as a serious experiment, you'll learn what works and what doesn't, as Edison did, and what might be possible if approached differently.

Doing Things Differently Produces Different Results

It's never too early in a job search to start thinking about how you'll market yourself. When you prepare a marketing strategy, you determine a method for letting the work world know you are here and what you can do. But it can't be a shotgun approach. It's important to target particular companies to approach that are within a specific business sector, such as manufacturing, banking, information technology, or communication, then determine the function you'll pursue, such as sales, human resources, business development, or account management. Once you determine which companies to approach, the next series of actions involves people contact. In chapter 7, you'll learn more about getting referrals through networking.

STRATEGIES FOR SUCCESS

By having a structure for recording and measuring your progress—and using it—you are likely to get a job faster, on average, than searchers who don't keep adequate track of what they are doing. Try it and see.

KEY IDEAS

1.

2.

3.

ACTION STEPS

1.

2.

3.

IMPLEMENTATION

1.

2.

3.

RESULTS

1.

2.

3.

By following this process, you've decided to differentiate yourself from other job hunters. You now have a powerful measure of control that can boost your confidence as you act on the self-efficacy belief that you can organize, coordinate, and direct your actions toward achieving a purposeful, meaningful, and measurable goal: a great new job.

POSTSCRIPT

Sometimes in life, you find yourself at a crossroads. Which direction do you take? What do you bring with you? How do you view where you are and where you are going? Though such general questions can be interesting to ponder, they also pave the procrastination path. Grabbing the air differs from grabbing the wheel.

There are endless questions you can ask yourself, but a well-articulated process question has the promise of a solution built into its structure: *To get a job at XYZ Corporation, what steps do I take, how do I take them, and when do I take them? If I make a consistent error by thinking "I'm in a powerless position and must trust the fates," then what steps do I take to examine the premises beneath this assumption, and when do I start?* Process questions and action steps open up a path to high adventure, where you learn more about what you can do. Travel that way if you dare.

2 PURSUE YOUR SEARCH WITH CLARITY AND STAMINA

Walt Kelly's cartoon strip *Pogo* (1943–1975) is a commentary on the human condition. Probably his most famous quote is the slogan first seen on his 1970 Earth Day poster: *We Have Met the Enemy and He Is Us.* Walt Kelly has not been with us for some time, and it's been several decades since this popular cartoon strip appeared weekly in newspapers throughout the world. Nevertheless, the idea that most people place unnecessary restrictions on themselves is as valid today as ever. This chapter will show you how to break away from needless restrictions, especially those imposed by unrealistic and negative thinking.

No one is exempt from self-doubts, unrealistic expectations, and other forms of counterfeit beliefs that fog the field of reality. During a job search, these consistent errors can take many forms, such as thinking that finding a job will be easy, that you shouldn't be in this current mess, or that you have all the time in the world to find a great job. Nevertheless, everyone who has a job got the job despite having human faults. But remaining weighted down by consistent errors will likely slow your progress. For example, if you doubt yourself and then allow yourself to get sidetracked by diversions (such as watching TV instead of creating a résumé), you are working against your own best interests.

To help you become a fearless job hunter, we'll introduce you to a powerful ABCDE psychological technique for boosting your effectiveness. In later chapters we'll show how this method can speed your search and reduce job stress. But before we get to that stage, let's start with Kathy's story.

➤ Kathy's Story

Kathy is a capable person who falls into a slump after losing her job. This forty-two-year-old accountant is the business manager of an automobile dealership that folds when a major auto manufacturer files for Chapter 11 bankruptcy. Before that happens, Kathy hopes for an economic recovery that doesn't come in time to save the business or her job.

Few initially take a job loss stoically, but Kathy's job loss really takes the wind out of her sails. She feels sad and worries about her coworkers' welfare, especially "Uncle Carl," who owns the dealership and treats everyone like a family member. Although she sounds upbeat when speaking with her dealership friends, even encouraging them to use their wonderful talents to get reemployed, she doesn't take her own advice. She feels stuck in apprehension about her future and powerless over what has come. A concerned Uncle Carl talks her into doing a fearless job search.

PESSIMISM AND PERFECTIONISM

Kathy believes she'll never find another great job, and this pessimistic view goes beyond the normal sadness experienced after a job loss. She faces the familiar enemy known as perfectionism, which gets in the way of her job search.

Tying her identity to her job, Kathy was more than fastidious in her work. She fretted about doing things perfectly, often triple-checking her work, which took extra time. To make sure she did things right, she was the first to get to work in the morning and the last to leave at night. Practically everyone, including Uncle Carl, kindly told her that good enough was good enough.

Kathy's consistent pessimism and perfectionism errors hold her back. She feels stuck with what she believes is a grim, jobless future. She thinks she must be perfect to qualify for a new job, which puts her in an impossible double mental bind: to get a job she needs to be perfect, and she isn't perfect, so she can't get a job. Although her conflict is fraudulent, her stressed emotions seem to confirm these two beliefs. People commonly use feelings to confirm their misperceptions.

Kathy initially accepts her feelings as her GPS, taking her pessimistic and perfectionistic beliefs for granted. So you can imagine how happy she is when she learns she can rethink her thinking and get on track to find a great new job. The next section tells how to do this.

THE ABCS OF PERSPECTIVE BUILDING

Rational emotive behavior therapy (REBT), pioneered by the great American psychologist Albert Ellis, is uniquely designed to help you deal with consistent psychological errors and regain control of your life. Learning and using this method may help you psychologically outdo your competitors for the job you want. Cutting through procrastination, thinking clearly and calmly, and energizing yourself to accomplish job-search tasks gives you a measurable edge. Plus, the confidence you gain in your abilities impresses interviewers.

Hundreds of research articles support REBT's effectiveness in reducing various complex forms of needless human distress (e.g., David et al. 2005). You can teach yourself to apply basic self-help ideas by using Ellis's (2003) famous ABCDE approach:

> *A* stands for an *adverse* activating event that merits resolution. An unwanted job loss and learning that someone else got the job you wanted qualify as adversities.

> *B* is how you think about, *believe* about, evaluate, or define A. This can be a dispassionate, fact-based, rational idea, or one that's erroneous or exaggerated. The more irrational beliefs that promote needless distress or interfere with productive efforts are of special interest. You can hamper your job search

by thinking that you are too fatigued to succeed, that others are in line before you in the search, or that you have to be absolutely sure of all facets of the search before you can do anything.

➢ *C* represents the emotional and behavioral *consequences*, or results, that extend from beliefs. In other words, it's the beliefs at B that greatly contribute to how you feel and act at C, not the adversities themselves at A.

➢ *D* stands for *disputing* or questioning beliefs associated with harmful emotions and ineffective actions. This approach can be as simple as following Socrates 101: define the belief, give examples, and give exceptions. A belief can't be true all the time if you can find exceptions.

➢ *E* stands for the new *effects* from questioning your self-defeating assumptions and resolving them in favor of a fact-based perspective.

Like Pogo's comment on human nature, the ABCDE approach applies across time and life themes to counteract your "enemy within." Once you understand this approach, you can profitably use it again and again.

Kathy's ABCs

Here's how Kathy uses the ABCDE approach to eliminate her consistent pessimism and perfectionism. Her A, or adverse activating event, is losing her job when the auto dealership she works for goes out of business. Her B, or consistent-error belief, is that she will never find another good job because she just isn't good enough, which is best exemplified by these two thoughts: *I'll never find another job to match this one, so basically it's all downhill for me from here* (pessimism). *I must be absolutely perfect in every conceivable way to qualify for a new job* (perfectionism). This combination of pessimistic and perfectionistic beliefs is linked to emotional and behavioral consequences, such as Kathy's C, or emotional consequence: feeling immobilized. The D part of Ellis's system is the GPS that gets her off a crooked path and back on track.

The D of Perspective Building

Our beliefs are normally functional. For example, self-efficacy is the belief that you can organize and direct your own actions. If your work hours are cut, you might correctly believe and rightly feel frustrated if this change hinders your economic goals and creates financial hardship.

You can gain momentum in your job search by using time and energy lost in consistent-error beliefs, emotions, and negative actions. You can make your life a lot easier. To defeat consistent-error beliefs, Ellis (2003) advocates disputing them and replacing them with fact-based beliefs.

SEVEN PERSPECTIVE-BUILDING QUESTIONS FOR
DISPUTING HARMFUL BELIEFS

By questioning consistent errors in belief, you engage the disputation process. But the type of questions you ask yourself can make a positive difference.

In the disputing phase, you apply critical thinking to the suspect belief. Here are some sample questions: *Would a reasonable person agree with this definition? Does this belief assume something's a fact? Is there a credible alternative way to view this situation? Is there confirmable evidence for the belief's validity? Can I treat this belief like a hypothesis and test it?*

You can also use a cookbook approach, where you apply a definition of rational thinking to the suspect belief that you associate with distress and ineffective actions. We've developed a set of questions that specifically fit a job search. Here's how the system works: ask yourself seven perspective-building questions that apply to both a suspected irrational belief and a suspected rational one concerning your job search.

SEVEN PERSPECTIVE-BUILDING QUESTIONS

Does My Belief...	Yes	No
1. Support reality because it's derived from fact?		
2. Advance my job-seeking goals and interests?		
3. Support quality relationships?		
4. Serve as a catalyst for positive actions and performance?		
5. Provide a wide range of healthy emotions?		
6. Promote healthy lifestyle habits?		
7. Result in openness and flexibility under changing conditions?		

By taking a disputation step, you position yourself to be unburdened from whatever slows your search, thereby narrowing the gap between where you are now and the job you seek. The following section shows how Kathy uses the distinction between functional and dysfunctional beliefs to challenge her negative job-seeking outlook. As you get more familiar with the process, you'll become proficient at defusing consistent-error beliefs, just as Kathy does.

Kathy's New Perspective

Kathy's ABCDE resolution example, which follows, shows how to distinguish between functional and dysfunctional beliefs to reduce your stress and support a "challenge" outlook toward seeking a great job. As you get more familiar with the process, there are many other ways to review your beliefs and defuse consistent errors that alter your perspective and churn up distress.

In the ABC phase, Kathy notices connections among her pessimistic beliefs, downtrodden feelings, and inertia about engaging in job-search activities. She is in a good position to take a close look at the validity of what she now recognizes as her erroneous consistent-error beliefs.

When Kathy gets to the D phase of this process, she applies the seven criteria for perspective building by answering each question as it applies to her pessimistic thinking. Discovering a fact-based perspective, she generates a new E, or effect. Here's how:

KATHY'S ABCDE RESOLUTION

A *Adverse* or activating event:	An unwanted job loss
B Consistent-error pessimistic *belief*:	"I'll never find another job to match this one, so basically it's all downhill from here."
C Emotional and behavioral *consequences* extending from consistent-error belief:	"I feel bummed out and have trouble getting started on the job search."

D *Disputing* (correcting) consistent-error belief:		
Question Does my belief...	Answer	E New *Effects*:
1. Support reality because it's derived from fact?	1. No, there's no evidence I can't find another great job. I've found excellent jobs in the past, so there's no reason to think I can't in the future.	1. There's reason for hope, so it makes sense to swing into action.

2. Advance my job-seeking goals and interests?	2. This negative outlook interferes with effective job-search performance by excluding success as a possibility.	2. Testing an assumption is better than following a dark tunnel that leads nowhere.
3. Support quality relationships?	3. Continuing in negativity will likely turn people off, making them less likely to be attracted to and help me.	3. Being confident I'll find a great new job will bring out my natural sparkle, drawing people to help me get what I want.
4. Serve as a catalyst for positive actions and performance?	4. The results speak for themselves. I do little that's constructive toward my job search and thus suffer.	4. Taking positive action by organizing, regulating, and directing my behavior might help me discover, or even positively impact, my future.
5. Provide a wide range of healthy emotions?	5. Thinking pessimistically limits my range of emotions to a dumpy mood.	5. While a down mood won't stop at my command, I can redirect my thinking toward what I *can* control, such as viewing my job loss in a different way and imagining myself applying my excellent accounting and management skills to a challenging new opportunity.

6. Promote healthy lifestyle habits?	6. Thinking pessimistically is an unhealthy lifestyle habit and a consistent but correctable error. It brings me down, which in turn negatively impacts my motivation to take care of myself and connect with friends and loved ones.	6. Fact-based beliefs provide a better alternative. Accepting a loss as irrevocable, and realizing that job skills don't vanish with the loss and that job stability isn't a birthright, puts a difficult situation into a manageable light. Further, the more I open to life, the better I'll be in my job search.
7. Result in openness and flexibility under changing conditions?	7. Definitely not! I associate this line of thought with being trapped in a rut.	7. I can choose to either let this thinking go unchecked or examine it. By choosing to analyze my pessimistic thinking, I've already opened myself to seeing my job loss and my job search differently. Maybe I can manage my expectations by keeping an open mind to alternatives.

Although Kathy soon gets past her pessimism, it isn't until a week later that her lingering down mood fully passes. As when dealing with any loss, time is an antidote. But Kathy feels an immediate sense of freedom when she realizes she can stop thinking pessimistically. She feels pleased to add to her coping self-efficacy by blowing away the fog of pessimism.

Kathy next tackles her perfectionistic thinking using the same ABCDE model. For example, she explores why her need for infallible performance seems to be a prerequisite for getting a job, and she concludes that no one would ever seek work if perfection really *were* a prerequisite. Released from perfectionistic thinking and with a clearer mind, Kathy carries out her fearless job hunting plan with the same diligence she showed on her previous job. She reviews her career objectives, prepares her résumé, and starts networking with people to get referrals to gatekeepers who could open the door to a great job. If she catches herself slumping, she takes corrective action by reapplying the ABCDE approach.

Does Kathy find a great new job? Her fearless job hunting program pays off, and she now serves as a manager for a midcap medical services company. She looks forward to going to work each day and has an active social life outside her job.

Your ABCDE Approach

Now it's your turn to use this same ABCDE approach to eliminate your own self-handicapping thoughts or beliefs that block your job-search path. Like Kathy, what you do first is identify the adversity you are facing (A), the consistent-error beliefs (B), and the emotional and behavioral consequences extending from your consistent-error beliefs that hold you back from getting your next great job (C). Then you rigorously question and dispute these unhealthy beliefs (D) and record the positive, energizing effect (E) of the disputation. Organizing the information this way gives you a sense of control over the process, which can lead to a welcome sense of relief and, ultimately, a reasonably faster-paced job search.

To help yourself find your consistent-error beliefs, you might want to consider the following typical thought errors often held by people who procrastinate on the job hunt:

> ➤ *Hopelessness:* "It'll never happen." "There's nothing out there for me." "There are too many job seekers and too few jobs to be had."

➤ *Self-doubt:* "My résumé (education, looks, experience, or IQ) doesn't stack up with others." "They'll probably overlook me." "What chance do I have, with all the superstars out there?"

➤ *Low frustration tolerance:* "It's too hard to have to go through all this hassle." "I can't stand all the BS that goes on in a job interview." "It's horrible to be put through all this malarkey."

➤ *All-or-none thinking:* "If I don't get a new job fast, I'll never get one." "I've got one chance and one chance only, so I'd better make the most of it." "If I fail at this interview, I'll probably fail at all future ones."

➤. *Self-perfectionism:* "I have to be perfect or else no one will want to hire me." "I must do perfectly in my interview."

➤ *Situational perfectionism:* "I have to have the perfect job or I couldn't bear it." "I have to have the perfect job for me." "Settling for less than the best is selling out."

➤ *Other perfectionism:* "There must be a perfect match between me and my prospective coworkers." "If the interviewer doesn't show me perfect respect, I'll just walk out the door." "I must be able to connect with my supervisor or else I'll just go nuts."

➤ *Phony self-labeling:* "Failing to land a decent job makes me a failure." "It's shameful to have to go through this job-search process." "At my age, being in the job market is a total humiliation."

Now it's time for you to do your first ABCDE resolution. Go back and review the material presented earlier in this chapter if you think a refresher will be helpful. Make copies of the following form to have on hand in your job-search work environment.

Your ABCDE Resolution

A *Adverse* or activating event:	
B Consistent-error pessimistic *belief*:	
C Emotional and behavioral *consequences* extending from consistent-error belief:	

D *Disputing* (correcting) consistent-error belief:		
Question Does my belief...	Answer	E New *Effects*
1. Support reality because it's derived from fact?		
2. Advance my job-seeking goals and interests?		
3. Support quality relationships?		
4. Serve as a catalyst for positive actions and performance?		
5. Provide a wide range of healthy emotions?		
6. Promote healthy lifestyle habits?		
7. Result in openness and flexibility under changing conditions?		

Extend the System

If the ABCDE method appeals to you, the following concept and application table describes some extensions of the system:

Concept	Application
Three dimensions of acceptance: Ellis promotes an attitude of acceptance, a scientific method of inquiry to solve life's problems, tolerate human frailties, and appreciate the unique characteristics of others and ourselves, resulting in an unconditional acceptance of self, others, and life (Ellis 2003).	Acceptance boils down to the fundamental concept that reality is what *is*, not what it *should* be.
Double trouble: People commonly contribute to their own troubles—for example, by feeling anxious over feeling anxious. This double trouble can amplify your distress and distract you from resolving problems, but it's correctable.	Viewing stress as a passing state makes any form of unwanted tension easier to tolerate.

The self as pluralistic: Unlike self-esteem, where you value yourself for what you do and what others may think of you, self-acceptance involves a broader view of self that takes into account how multifaceted you are and the impossibility of generalizing from a single behavior to a whole self.	Giving yourself a global rating for losing or landing a job is an overgeneralization, like declaring yourself a winner or loser, good or bad, smart or a dunce. You can, and would wisely, judge your behavior, not yourself. So, you may act badly in a situation or fail at something, but *you*—meaning your whole self—are never all good or all bad, unless you foolishly decide by decree to make it that way.
Homework assignments: All your life, you've learned by doing. For example, you may read about how to drive a car, but until you get behind the wheel, you won't get a real understanding of how to drive under different conditions. Ellis's behavioral, or homework, assignments involve actively engaging with a problem to gain experience in resolving it.	If you fear choking during an interview, put yourself through the paces of a dozen dry runs until your tension subsides. This form of *exposure therapy* is the gold standard for fighting and overcoming fear. It's also a basic technique for testing beliefs and assumptions, and for building durable skills, such as assertiveness and social skills.

FREE YOURSELF FROM PROCRASTINATION-THINKING TRAPS

Procrastination is an automatic habit of putting off a timely and important action until another day or time. This process always involves some form of diversion, such as calling friends, surfing the Internet—anything but dealing with the pressing priority. The process practically always includes various forms of mental diversion or procrastination thinking, such as "I'll need to wait a while," "I'll get to this tomorrow," and "I'll do it after I do more research" (and then you put off the research).

A whisper of negative emotion can trigger this complex process, and it can billow from there. Even the perception that a task is complex can trigger it, as well as feeling discouraged or doubtful or having excessively high expectations. And while it's not your fault you acquired this habit, it's your responsibility to take corrective action when procrastination interferes with your job search.

In this section we'll look at three forms of procrastination thinking: counterfactual thinking, self-handicapping, and the "later" illusion. Applying the seven perspective-building questions to these forms of thinking gives you a quick perspective on its self-defeating nature. We'll give you additional ways to quell each thinking distraction. Because this complex process can interfere so much with your job search, throughout the book we'll give you multiple ways to follow up efficiently and effectively on productive job-search initiatives. (If you are interested in learning about comprehensive programs to curb procrastination, see *The Procrastination Workbook: Your Personalized Program for Breaking Free from the Patterns That Hold You Back* (New Harbinger Publications, 2002) and *End Procrastination Now! Get It Done with a Proven Psychological Approach* (McGraw-Hill, in press), by William Knaus.

Get Out of the Counterfactual Trap

Melody goes job hunting after her bank is taken over in a hostile merger with a larger firm, which results in her being let go. At first she feels shocked and dismayed; then she endures self-questioning and self-doubts. She occupies herself by thinking, "I should have seen this coming. I should have taken the XYZ Company job offer last year when I had the chance." This is called *counterfactual thinking*, because it's not true (Epstude and Roese 2008).

You may have noticed yourself thinking about what you could or should have done. While highly common, counterfactual thinking tends to lead to self-recrimination. When you allow your anxious feelings to lead you to engage in this form of thinking, you are more likely to procrastinate (Sirois 2004).

If you fall into this thinking trap, awareness is a positive step in the direction of liberation. Here's a reality perspective: What happened happened, and all the "could haves" in the world won't change that reality. Now, what can you do to take advantage of what you learned and apply it to the present?

Get Out of the Self-Handicapping Trap

You tell yourself the job market's too tight for you to stand a chance of getting a good job. You tell yourself you are too bummed out to start your job search now. You tell yourself your finances are in jeopardy, so you can't concentrate on your search now. What do these statements have in common? All are forms of *self-handicapping*.

Engaging in self-handicapping sets up obstacles to justify delays. The excuses serve a double purpose: they justify delay and excuse weak results, saving your self-esteem. After all, it's not your fault if you operate under handicapping conditions. But self-handicapping is a red herring, an intellectual distraction that shifts attention from the real issue, which may be fear of failure, discomfort over uncertainty, or something as simple as not knowing what to do at first. Self-handicapping is strongly associated with procrastination (van Eerde 2003) and lower production (Beck, Koons, and Milgrim 2000), and when it co-occurs with counterfactual thinking, performance improvements are less likely (McCrea 2008).

If you catch yourself engaging in this form of procrastination thinking, that's good news. You can change faulty thinking.

Get Out of the Tomorrow-Thinking Trap

Is mañana good enough for you? If so, you may have handicapped yourself by thinking later is better. This *later* thinking is a cognitive signature of procrastination that comes in many subvarieties, such as "I'll get started on my job search when I feel inspired."

Some actions *are* best to do later—after preparatory efforts. It's wiser to think through how to approach gatekeepers than to randomly call potential contacts and make it up as you go. But letting delay statements substitute for productive actions is waylaying yourself.

If you catch yourself engaged in this mañana, or tomorrow, thinking, what's behind the delay? In many instances you'll find an emotional motivation for the idea. Preferring to avoid discomfort, you hope that by delaying, you'll have no consequences. Here's a reality perspective: unless you have compelling evidence that putting it off till tomorrow will provide opportunities that are superior to starting now, assume that you are engaging in procrastination thinking. Ask yourself, what are the consequences of putting off a timely and important action, and what are the consequences of following through now? Compare the results. Note that when you follow through effectively, your self-efficacy beliefs and productive actions are likely to yield quality results.

In chapter 3, you'll find a framework for making a formal cost-benefit analysis of delayed versus purposeful and timely actions. The next section will show you how to boost your frustration tolerance for following through.

QUICK TIPS

➤ When feeling distressed about an unpleasant event, think about your thinking. That may be the real source of your adversity.

➤ Organize your emotionally charged experiences so you can see the connections among evocative events, your thoughts, your feelings, and your behavioral responses, and you'll introduce a constructive change into the process.

➤ Work on building your emotional "muscles" by teaching yourself to accept the inevitable frustrations in life and then by controlling what you can.

➤ Prefer action over intellectual analysis when the action allows you to alter your perspective with new, fact-based beliefs.

FRUSTRATION-TOLERANCE TRAINING

Developing a high frustration tolerance is one of the most underrated, yet probably most important, areas for self-improvement (Knaus 1983). Here, you boost your ability to withstand the ordinary and extraordinary frustrations and stresses of life. With a high frustration tolerance, you are likely to feel amused in the same situations that cause others to fly off the handle with little provocation, quit important projects when challenged, and experience intense impatience when required to wait.

Most needless human stress derives from an unwillingness to tolerate stress, tension, and frustration, as well as magnifying and intensifying them by focusing too much on them. We'll introduce you to methods to boost your tolerance for frustration and related tension so you can better meet frustrating job-search challenges. Boosting your tolerance for unpleasant situations and sensations may result in less stress.

If frustration-tolerance training interests you, we've made available a free e-book, *How to Conquer Your Frustrations* (Knaus 1983). It has the unique feature of intentionally being written with minimal use of the verb "to be," an approach that reduces overgeneralizing and simultaneously (but subtly) teaches clear-thinking skills. You can download this free book at www.rebtnetwork.org/library/How_to_Conquer_Your_Frustrations.pdf.

Recognize Low Frustration Tolerance

Blocked goals commonly result in frustration. Within a moderate range, frustration can motivate you toward higher levels of performance. But a tendency toward intolerance for frustration can negatively affect positive performance when the tasks you face tend to be complex. Low frustration tolerance (LFT) may have the single most negative impact on an otherwise successful job search. Because of this risk, LFT merits attention and resolution, so we'll show you how to do that next.

Low frustration tolerance is a tendency to run away from tension without much forethought. It can be an adaptive reaction when it triggers actions directed at getting something done. But this reaction can also trigger procrastination—for example, when you have an urge to divert from job-search activities and dodge your discomfort by searching the Web for information about old friends or by recalling negative situations. Focusing on the onerous aspects of a situation can also distract you from your job search. As you stay stuck in this spot, your most pressing and important job-search activities get put onto the back burner. It's easy to see how, in the low-frustration-tolerance mode of emotion-driven thinking, you are likely to create other frustrations for yourself. Acting impetuously, avoiding important but uncomfortable job-search actions, rushing through writing your résumé—all may result in added frustrations and duplicated efforts to repair the damage.

LFT awareness is positive, meaning you can do something to change it if you recognize it. For example, by labeling low-frustration thinking and behaviors, you make them understandable, and understanding something is a form of control. You are now in a catbird's seat to see what's going on and to get past this stumbling block as you pursue your job-search goals.

Frustrations morph into low frustration tolerance when you amplify the negativity in a job search. This amplification comes about by how you evaluate your situation. If you judge the tension you experience in your job search as awful or intolerable, this labeling will amplify your stress. Recognizing this amplification process is the first step on the path to building high frustration tolerance and enjoying the accomplishments you gain from this resilience in the face of tension.

LFT can be a default reaction to anything you experience as uncomfortable. Here, the solution is to refuse to divert from the problem and squarely face it. But this is rarely simple or easy, because it's easy to fail to recognize when LFT is a default reaction and take quick corrective action, and often you'll find additional complications. Because LFT often follows definable steps, we observe these highly common variations on the process:

1. You feel frustrated when you perceive that your goals are out of reach for now.

2. You occupy yourself with the gap between where you are and where you want to be.

3. You tell yourself that you can't stand not having what you want when you want it.

4. You exaggerate and dramatize the horrors of your situation.

While we hope you don't fall into the LFT trap during your job search, the good news is that you can contest it and reduce it. So, if you find yourself in this trap, as millions often do, how do you make a strategic exit?

LFT is a self-absorbing process where you focus attention on your tensions and what you think are the causes, which is like putting a magnifying glass over a leaf, allowing the sun to ignite it. This magnification of tension can expand to a fear of feeling tense and procrastinating to avoid the dread of tension.

You can ditch your tension magnifier by making the radical shift to a self-observant perspective. When in a self-observant perspective, you act to build an objective perspective by developing a rational understanding and finding solutions to the important problems you want to solve. To get to this perspective, you step outside of yourself.

Free Yourself from the LFT Trap

If you are like most people, you are inclined to focus your attention on troublesome situations. Here, you risk falling into thinking that the situation is at fault and that the solution is to change what may be outside of your control, such as a job loss.

How you normally perceive and evaluate situations affects how you feel or respond. So, in a self-observant way, you should shift from focusing on tension to thinking about your thinking. This form of self-monitoring is called *metacognitive thinking*. Few people do this, and still fewer do it well. But identifying stress-amplifying LFT thoughts puts you in a position to change them.

When you suspect you are experiencing LFT, apply the seven criteria for an objective perspective. For example, if you declare yourself powerless to effect change, it's useful to know why, where, and whether this is a reality or if you could try another way. If it's a reality, such as another person got the job you wanted, so be it. By self-observantly attacking problems (not yourself), you'll more likely experience a high and durable sense of self-confidence that's grounded to your competent actions.

The following table describes three types of LFT self-talk—exaggerated exasperations, urgency phrases, and avoidance phrases—and how to meet them with self-observant corrective action.

LFT Self-Talk	Self-Observant Action Perspective
Exaggerated exasperations: "This is too much for me."	Look for opportunities to break down a complex job-search problem, and start to work at generating solutions. This radical shift promotes a sense of control.
Urgency phrases: "I can't stand this. I must stop feeling stressed right now."	Intolerance is a mental evaluation that distracts you from meeting challenges. To promote a healthier perspective, apply the seven perspective questions to the belief that you can't stand the situation. You might also ask yourself why you think tension is intolerable.
Avoidance phrases: "I can't do this."	The power of negation can be alluring, much like the sirens of Greek mythology who lured sailors to crash their ships on the shore. Rather than using a blanket negation, look for opportunities and challenges in the process.

By making purposeful, self-observant efforts to pursue your job search, you gain a triple positive: stronger coping self-efficacy, reduced negatives from a self-absorbent process, and more time and resources to put into productive job-search pursuits.

THREE STEPS TO A HIGH FRUSTRATION TOLERANCE

Developing a high frustration tolerance has benefits—for example, you are likely to show a quiet, calm competence in an interview, because when you are in command of yourself, you can better command the events taking place around you. There are many ways to raise your tolerance, but the following three-phase frustration-tolerance training program gives a tested buffer against needless stress and a solid platform from which to build effective self-observant problem-solving capabilities.

> *Build your body* to buffer yourself against pressures from multiple ongoing frustrations. Get regular exercise; follow a healthy diet; maintain a reasonable weight for your gender, height, and age; and get adequate sleep. This buffering process reduces what Rockefeller University professor Bruce McEwen calls the *allostatic load factor*, or wear and tear on the body due to multiple stresses (McEwen and Lasley 2007). Ongoing stress increases the risk of disease, fatigue, and mood disorders, so building the body has an added value in reducing these risks.

> *Liberate the mind* from consistent errors that promote ongoing stress. This liberation includes dealing with self-defeating thinking as well as low frustration tolerance self-talk, such as telling yourself things like "I can't take this" and "I must have relief right now." A core psychological antidote to this type of thinking is to establish a sense of control, which you can do by mastering the ABCDE approach. We urge you to build an ABCDE resolution process into your daily routine. As the ancient Greeks preached, a sound mind in a sound body is the key to well-being and productivity.

> *Change patterns* you associate with needless frustrations, such as holding back from going after what you want, avoiding contention at all costs, inhibiting yourself from engaging in the normal pursuit of happiness, or following a path of general disorganization. Work toward developing the naturalness of thought and action that comes from believing you can cope effectively and operate competently in your life's work. This fact-based belief comes from developing your capabilities through self-observant efforts to think and act effectively.

STRATEGIES FOR SUCCESS

Few things in life are more important than your command of yourself and what you do in your life. A pattern of self-efficacy, self-acceptance, and frustration tolerance characterizes a life well lived.

KEY IDEAS

1.

2.

3.

ACTION PLAN

1.

2.

3.

IMPLEMENTATION

1.

2.

3.

RESULTS

1.

2.

3.

POSTSCRIPT

As long as you are conscious, you can develop your intellect, innovativeness, and initiative to select where you work and how you can meet your future employer's job objectives. You have the option of establishing command over what you think and do. This revolutionary idea is based on the premise that you can generate different perspectives about an event because there are often different ways to look at a situation. If you don't like how you think, try another way.

3 OPTIMIZE YOUR JOB-SEARCH PERFORMANCE

Have you ever wished you could call upon your best resources on demand? Wouldn't you love to be able to perform like a top professional golfer, who seems to almost always hit his drive onto the fairway or sink that ten-foot putt when needed?

How do the professionals so frequently rise to the occasion? How do they make it look so easy? They have unusual talent and, thus, rapid money-producing skills. What we don't see is the long, hard practice and preparation that helps them deliver in the clutch. In short, behind the scenes they work long and hard at what seems to come easily.

The value of reflective preparation has been passed down through the ages. Highly successful organizations build on platforms of preparation. Indeed, the nineteenth-century Prussian military strategist Carl von Clausewitz (1968 [1832]) emphasized that preparation counted above all else prior to an engagement. He thought the decisions you make during the conflict often result from your preparatory activities.

In chapters 1 and 2 we looked at tactics that support a successful job-search strategy. The tactics involve reducing consistent errors that promote distractions that can interfere with a successful job search. Use these methods to support maximum performance when it's important to operate at your best.

We'll share four high-powered tactics to optimize your job-search performance, starting with *using language of committed action* to shape your career direction. Next we'll introduce you to *the power of passionate purpose* to energize your job-search challenges. The next step along the path of ending procrastination interferences is learning how to *leverage pleasure and pain*, which involves exploring the pleasure principle. Finally, we'll round out the program with *optimal performance training*. Combined, these four job-search tactics can help prepare you psychologically to make the most of the opportunities that lie before you.

USE THE LANGUAGE OF COMMITTED ACTION

The language you use when you talk to yourself represents your knowledge, your beliefs, how you feel, and what you do. If you believe you can handle the unknowns that lie before you, and if you tell yourself you'll prevail come what may, you are already on your way to a successful job search. Thus, how you talk yourself through this process can make the difference.

Words have power. You translate what you know, believe, and feel through the words you use to describe your perceived realities. Your thoughts and words are tied to what you do. When you harness your language to energize, regulate, and advance your job search, you smartly position yourself to move forward.

Listen to what you tell yourself when you make a commitment to advancing your search. Do you hedge by saying "I'll probably get to this later"? If you need to prepare for an upcoming interview and tell yourself you will probably review information about the company later, that's a weak commitment to action. If you tell yourself, "I'm hopping on the computer now to search for company information," this use of action words shows a strong commitment. You've backed up the task with a firm commitment to action by acting in a "no delay" time frame.

A commitment amounts to integrity, and the key underlying concept is the implied trust that you'll keep your word. We're talking about a commitment to keep your word as a fundamental character principle. But what if you make the commitment to you? Do you have greater latitude to backtrack, or do you have a responsibility to keep your word to yourself? If you keep your word to yourself, you'll likely act responsibly when you commit to an action. You'll sprint ahead of your competitors who don't take their self-commitments seriously. Acting as if your word to yourself is worth as much as a bald tire puts you on the slippery slope to procrastination.

In committing to a fearless job search, are you willing to take extra steps to do the necessary homework on companies where you'd like to work? Are you willing to improve your communication and interview skills? Are you prepared to sharpen your ability to negotiate when you receive a job offer? If not, you are operating on hope, not on committed action. Since commitments take extra work, it's wise to commit only to what you'll follow through with.

You can hear a commitment with integrity in a firm statement such as "I'm very determined to do this." You hear a cold commitment in an irresolute "I think I'll get around to this" or "I'll try to do this sometime." When you make a strong commitment to change, that change will more likely take place if you work to resolve any ambiguity you have about the purpose of your search, which is to get a great job. Reducing such ambiguities is associated with positive change (Hodgins, Ching, and McEwen 2009). However, a commitment to carry out a specific plan will ordinarily get you farther than making a general commitment to change.

A plan defines the steps you'll take to achieve the goal you chose to undertake. A better plan includes specific activities and, sometimes, due dates for completing segments of the plan. To work harder, for example, isn't a useful plan. Noting how you'll work harder by doing what where and when is better. A commitment to action that includes a start time and a self-determined but realistic deadline is normally a hot action, whereas a commitment to "work harder" is normally a cold thought.

A written commitment is typically hotter than a verbal one. Use the following table to define what you are willing to commit to do to advance your job search and how you plan to get there:

Commitment to Action	Action Plan
1.	1.
2.	2.

3.	3.
4.	4.
5.	5

The previous exercise fits snugly with von Clausewitz's principle of preparation and that of self-efficacy.

THE POWER OF PASSIONATE PURPOSE

We divide work into three levels. Level 1 work is when you view what you do as just a job. A level 1 job can be anything from building houses to selling life insurance to doing brain surgery. It's something you do to pay the bills, but you have little personal identification with it and virtually no burning passion to do it.

If you see yourself as engaged in a career, you are in level 2 work. You identify with your role as an engineer, a teacher, a psychologist, a steelworker, or whatever your job function is. In addition to making a good living, you likely feel motivated to achieve success in your career, maintain a positive reputation, belong to a peer group of colleagues with similar interests, and provide a quality product or service to customers or clients. Motivation to work is understandably higher for level 2 than level 1. So, your motivation to get a level 2 job is higher.

Level 3 work is an expression of your life's purpose. If you are at level 3, you are among a highly select group, but one that can significantly expand, because practically anyone can join this seemingly exclusive group.

If you are outside of the level 3 group and want to join, your preparation for this process can first range from random efforts to precise thinking and preparation. Random efforts are typically fruitless. Precise thinking and preparation is generally your hottest GPS approach, where you think through what fits you that has a meaningful purpose. Then you intentionally figure how to drive this purpose through your work. Few people achieve this level, primarily because few pursue it.

The power of passionate purpose has to do with reflecting on your life's purpose and is partially based on the seminal work of Stephen Covey (1989) in *The 7 Habits of Highly Effective People*. Approaching this challenge will help you add to your chances of reaping three added values through your work:

> - You bring passion, dedication, and determination to work each day, and you benefit from the by-product of your passion-driven efforts.

> - With daily enthusiasm for work, you increase your chances of continually improving the results you feel pride in achieving.

> - You feel deeply rewarded, satisfied, and fulfilled in your work because, after all, what you do on the job has deep meaning for you. If you are happy in your work, this tends to spread to other areas of your life.

Anyone can attain the power of passionate purpose, but it requires special effort and some acts of courage. Here are five famous individuals we believe contributed to their communities through their power of passionate purpose, which is likely the reason they achieved eminence without achieving great fortune:

> - You don't have to look far to see clarity in the minds of people who passionately pursue a vision or dream. Abraham Lincoln's "a house divided against itself cannot stand" speech defined his presidency. Though Lincoln suffered from depression, this disabling condition did not dissuade him from his purpose.

> - Duke University's men's basketball team, under coach Mike Krzyzewski, is a perennial ACC and NCAA championship contender. Krzyzewski sees his life's purpose not as coaching basketball, but as leading his student athletes to become good students, people, and citizens. The game is the means by which he achieves this.

> - India's great leader Mahatma Gandhi saw his life's purpose as living fearlessly to contest injustice and conquer untruth, even when these actions required suffering. In dedicating himself

to this purpose, Gandhi successfully led his nation to independence from Great Britain.

➤ Martin Luther King, Jr.'s "I Have a Dream" speech, which he delivered at the foot of the Lincoln Memorial in Washington, D.C., on August 28, 1963, brilliantly captures his life's purpose of achieving equality for all, where people are judged by their deeds, not by their color. Dr. King's purpose brought passion to each of his days. Despite ongoing obstacles, he continued to march forward to reach his goal of racial equality.

➤ Albert Ellis worked approximately eighteen hours a day for over fifty years to develop and advance rational emotive behavior therapy. He donated millions of dollars to the institute he founded and took a mere twelve thousand dollars a year as salary for several decades. At the age of ninety-two, he continued with extraordinary productivity. Ellis's energy was driven by his passionate purpose. This lifestyle is reserved for the few with such a single-minded purpose.

These five people clearly had articulated a purpose for a life's work. Out of that purpose, they acted with passion to create magnificent results. But you don't have to be a high-profile person like Lincoln or King to passionately pursue your life's purpose. Whether a carpenter, watercolor painter, or people's advocate, by connecting your life's purpose to meaningful work, you can generate energy and motivation that becomes self-perpetuating. By connecting purpose to your desired job, you also generate the passion you need to find that job.

Reflect and Act on Your Purpose

The power of passionate purpose is not like a lightbulb that illuminates when you twist it into place. This *passion* can be born of harsh experience as much as of insight and inspiration. A whistle-blower who was once a yes-person may rise to the occasion after a crisis in conscience from an awakening sense of fairness and justice. Without a war between the states, Lincoln's presidency would have been remarkably different.

If you are interested in exploring the concept of passionate purpose, here's a two-step process to help you. It starts with four questions to stimulate an inner dialogue. Your answers can help put you in touch with your deeper values and purpose.

Question of Purpose	Answer of Purpose
1. What absorbs my interest and attention that I find challenging to do?	
2. What are my unique qualities?	
3. What are my deepest values?	
4. What work activities do I most passionately pursue?	

Armed with your responses, develop a rough draft of your purpose. Keep it brief and positive, but make sure it represents a solid connection with your deepest values, desires, and capabilities. Reflect on it for about a week and then write the final version.

Once you have created your purpose, you are ready for the second step, which is to envision how you can express your purpose through the great new job you are seeking. We, for example, see this book as an opportunity to fulfill our purpose of enhancing the lives of the people we serve in our psychological and consulting work. Ask yourself, "In getting this great new job, what opportunities will there be to express my life's purpose, thereby producing results? Will I be proud of and feel deeply satisfied with each workday?"

PURPOSE AND FINANCIAL WORTH

You can find dignity and purpose in all forms of productive work. But does what you earn have a bearing on happiness? It may. If you earn less than twenty thousand dollars, you may experience more stress in life and less happiness. However, this was hardly the case with Albert Ellis, who voluntarily took less to build his institute so that it would survive beyond his death.

Once someone is beyond the point of earning a comfortable living, there's no meaningful difference in happiness between someone earning fifty thousand dollars annually and someone earning five hundred thousand. Income increases seem to have little lasting effect on happiness (Kahneman et al. 2006). But you do have more options with more money.

Earnings may be a good performance measure, but they are not a realistic measure of your global worth. If you feel that your worth depends on your earnings, you will likely fall into the contingent-worth trap. If you are out of work, your self-worth can plummet. The contingent-worth trap has more than one exit: one is to see yourself as multifaceted, and another is to take an action perspective.

LEVERAGE PLEASURE AND PAIN

For a moment, let's go back to Pogo's view that our worst problems originate from ourselves. Who is the "enemy within" us? As it turns out, our enemy may be a natural tendency that's sometimes out of place in the modern world: our tendency to seek pleasure and avoid pain, and to sacrifice a fulfilling future for specious rewards.

The pleasure principle is part of Sigmund Freud's description of our human tendency to avoid pain. But sometimes a whisper of negative emotion signals the primitive brain to retreat, when the wiser strategy is to advance.

Freud's horse-and-rider metaphor (1947) takes to a higher level the distinction between choosing a long-term gain and choosing a quick fix. You can use this metaphor when choosing among what would amount to a job that merely pays the rent or mortgage (level 1), a career (level 2), and a passion-driven vocation (level 3).

The horse symbolizes the easy path. The horse seeks immediate gratification and avoidance of discomfort or pain, an approach to living that makes horse sense in the short run. Enjoy today's simple pleasures and stay away from the dangers of the moment. There's ample room in life for such simple pleasures. But you have the gift of foresight along with the abilities to communicate, plan for the future, strategize, create, record history—and the list goes on. The rider symbolizes these higher-order cognitive functions. As the rider, you use your special gifts to delay immediate gratification and create your future.

The horse and rider are divisible but inseparable. With immediate gratification, the horse more often goes its own way, and the rider tags along. With delayed gratification, the rider more often holds the reins and goes in the direction of longer-term gain and prosperity.

The horse and rider are a team. Nevertheless, the conflict between the horse's brain and that of the level-headed rider is a constant issue.

The horse-and-rider metaphor points to a never-ending choice between grabbing short-term gains and aiming for greater long-term benefits. Psychological research abounds with studies involving people of all ages, and even monkeys and pigeons, repeatedly showing that most creatures choose small short-term gains over larger future gains. This strong tendency partially explains why you may delay pursuing a major priority where the payoff is in the distance. Substituting a trivial pursuit, if it has a brief marginal reward, appeals to the horse.

The horse is into expediency, rushing toward immediate pleasure without using reflective reason. Typically, hurried efforts spoil the long-range result.

An informed rider steps back and considers the current position and the desired goal. Sadly, this reflective process is a too easily skipped step, and its omission may partially explain why so many people dwell on problems without taking planned steps to solve them.

Quality solutions normally require preparatory actions that often take more time to conjure than to execute. For example, preparing for a job search takes a lot more time than interviewing and negotiating a job offer. Yet quality job-search preparation opens more gates to work opportunities.

The power of passionate purpose means harnessing the positive powers of emotion and motivation to gain passion and prosperity. But if you want to optimize your passionate pursuit, step back and compare your horse-and-rider options. This additional, reflective step is infrequently taken. We'll describe how a two-step cost-benefit analysis advances this process.

Follow-through is perhaps the most significant factor in a job search. Going for short-term benefits is a systemic risk that works against passionate purposes, higher-level accomplishments, and the happiness that comes as a by-product of productive activities. The following sample cost-benefit analysis will help you compare delaying to following through.

SAMPLE JOB-SEARCH COST-BENEFIT ANALYSIS

Job-Search Course of Action	Costs (Pain)	Benefits (Pleasure)
Horse Approach: Taking hasty actions, cutting corners, avoiding uncertainties, diverting to safe but nonproductive activities, avoiding the hard work it takes	1. Potentially compromises my ability to get a job 2. Limits my responsibility to find the job of my dreams 3. Makes me feel down on myself 4. Irritates my significant other 5. Perpetuates my financial distress	1. Takes less time, thought, and effort 2. Gives me immediate gratification 3. Helps me avoid discomfort 4. Helps me avoid the risk of failing 5. Lets me engage in hobbies and other pleasurable pursuits

Rider Approach: Using foresight, researching, persisting, following through, correcting consistent errors, exploring fit between talent and career direction, preparing résumés and cover letters, reviewing networking and interviewing options, getting my story to the right people, closing the deal, carrying over to the job what I learned during the search process	1. Takes significant time, thought, and effort 2. Deprives me of some readily available, immediate pleasures 3. Forces me to face some of my limitations 4. Can bring rejection	1. Develops strong self-regulation skills in tandem with advancing my self-efficacy skills (sometimes known as *inner control*) 2. Helps me move through the job search with thoughtful and planned actions 3. Establishes high frustration tolerance 4. Helps me operate with a broad range of talents that get developed through this process 5. Increases my opportunities to engage in a great career or passionate pursuit

Now it's your turn to do a cost-benefit analysis. In completing your lists, consider the painful elements and the benefits. Consult with family members who know you well and with trusted colleagues and friends. Others can add valuable refinements to your analysis.

As you fill in the following table, record specific examples, as in the sample table. Under "Horse Approach," describe what you do when you follow this approach, such as watch TV or bicker with your mate—anything that shows a hasty solution to divert you from a job-search challenge. Under "Rider Approach," describe what you do to advance your job search that has long-term benefits, such as reviewing résumé creation methods, crafting a résumé, and getting feedback from knowledgeable and trusted friends.

YOUR JOB-SEARCH COST-BENEFIT ANALYSIS

Job-Search Course of Action	Costs (Pain)	Benefits (Pleasure)
Horse Approach:		
Rider Approach:		

Once you have done your cost-benefit analysis, you are halfway home. If you are like most people whose horse is in control, how you associate pleasure and pain works against you—that is, you associate pleasure with immediate, short-term behavior, and you associate pain with delaying immediate gratification for long-term gain.

You can purposely connect doing hard work to pleasure and connect chasing short-term, immediate gratification to pain by going over it daily, which will motivate you to do the hard work and to resist the avoidant, distracting, self-absorbing behaviors that can sabotage your search. Now you have not only the cost-benefit analysis in place but also a sound reason to let the rider conduct the job search.

We've effectively used the cost-benefit analysis with all kinds of people, from those with severe drug and alcohol problems to chief executive officers considering starting a new business venture. Apply it to your job search and see if you can get the job you want. Your horse will also be satisfied with this result.

OPTIMAL PERFORMANCE TRAINING

Optimal performance training (OPT) is a psychological method for putting yourself in a "winning" state of mind. Originating in Germany around the turn of the twentieth century, the technique is used by many U.S. sports psychologists with superstar athletes (Olympic sports psychologist Gregory Raiport, personal communication). The Soviet Union also employed it during the 1976 Olympics (ibid.), and William Knaus adapted the approach to show how to boost short-term maximum-performance efforts in work settings (see *How to Get Out of a Rut*, published by Prentice-Hall, 1982).

OPT involves relaxation, mobilization, and action. During the relaxation stage, you use relaxing words and images to bring yourself to a state of relaxation. Next you connect words you associate with your prior peak performances with mobilizing for action. Then you move on to peak-performance actions. OPT yields advantages when it's important to present yourself in a calm and confident manner while networking, interviewing, and negotiating for a job.

Relax Your Body

In chapter 2 you learned how negative words and images can stir negative feelings. The words you use can also stir pleasurable and positive feelings. Does the thought of floating in a tub of warm, bubbly water stir a pleasurable feeling? Does the image of a drop from a ripe, juicy strawberry on your tongue evoke a pleasurable taste in your mouth? Similarly, you can learn to use words to recall memories of relaxation, and these images can promote relaxation in your body.

In the following exercise, we'll connect key words to relaxation sensations and then use the same words to evoke those desired sensations on command. Here's how to start this process: Take a shower and adjust the water so that it's comfortably warm. Step out of the way of the water

61

and let it flow only over your arms. Close your eyes and slowly repeat this phrase several times: "My arms are warm." Then do the same for your legs. Try this for several consecutive days. When you have associated the word "warm" with the warm, relaxing sensation of the water, think the word "warm" after each relaxation phrase. This helps cement a connection between the sensation of the warm shower, with its deepening state of relaxation, and the word "warm."

After the shower:

1. Lie down on your back and place a heavy pillow on your right arm. Make sure your body is comfortable and in a relaxed position.

2. Slowly take a deep breath and think the word "heavy" for about four seconds. As you continue to think the word "heavy," hold your breath for four seconds and exhale for four seconds until you have expelled all the air from your lungs. Then wait four seconds before you breathe in, repeating this cycle four times.

3. Close your eyes and concentrate your attention on the heaviness of your right arm. While concentrating on the weight of the pillow resting on your arm, say the phrase, "My arm feels heavy." Now do the same exercise for your legs.

Repeat this exercise three times a day for three days. Chances are you'll begin to feel a deepening sense of muscular and mental relaxation as you progress through this process. Then you are ready for the final part of the relaxation phase.

Now position yourself comfortably—preferably on your back, with outstretched arms, palms down. Close your eyes and repeat each relaxation phrase four times slowly and silently to yourself while concentrating on the sensations it suggests:

1. *My right arm is becoming warm and heavy.*

2. *Both my arms are becoming warm and heavy.*

3. *My legs are becoming warm and heavy.*

4. *I am resting.*

The relaxation phase has added benefits: You can use this process to restore your energy and feel refreshed and rested within a reasonably short time. Also, a relaxed body tends to stimulate positive, flexible, and productive thinking. Once you are working at your chosen job, you can fall back on relaxation when you need to put yourself into a mind-set of thinking "outside the box" to solve a problem.

Mobilize Your Mind

In the OPT mobilization phase, you create a healthy, action-oriented *peak performance experience* frame of mind and take action from it. You do this by connecting four phrases with an optimal performance state you've experienced. Similar to relaxation-imagery training, here, using your memories of an optimal performance, you develop the content to mobilize yourself. You find these phrases by tapping your memory for times in your life when you had an optimal performance experience. An optimal performance experience need not be the oneness with the universe that comes from the passive awareness of a surrounding experience. It's a by-product of a highly focused and impactful action. Four phrases describe the mobilization phase, where the sequence helps advance a felt sense of momentum. Here's a set of phrases that might capture the essence of an optimal performance experience when you're facing the difficult challenge of trying to hit the bull's-eye of a distant target.

1. *My eyes are fixed on the target.*

2. *My thoughts and the movements are one.*

3. *I direct my energy toward the target.*

4. *My actions and I are one.*

Here's a set of phrases that might help you express your thoughts with unusual clarity to capture the essence of a peak performance:

1. *I am in harmony with myself.*

2. *I am expressing my thoughts clearly.*

3. *My truth is in my words.*

4. *My words and I are one.*

The following mobilization phrases might facilitate a peak performance experience in selling a product:

1. *I am charged with energy.*

2. *I feel tingly.*

3. *My energy seeks expression.*

4. *I act with confidence.*

When connected to a real-life peak performance experience, mobilization phrases move you beyond a relaxed state to an energized one that may be especially valuable before you engage in important job-search communications.

Now, it's your turn to create your own set of mobilization phrases. Here are some guidelines: keep each phrase short (about six words or fewer); limit the number of phrases to four; make each statement positive; and see that it "flows" naturally and easily. Here are the steps to creating your phrases:

1. *Recall an optimal performance experience.* This could be when you swam farther than you thought you could, were engrossed in the act of skiing down a slope, spoke to a friend and experienced a strong sense of mutual understanding, wrote a poem that said what you wanted to say, solved a difficult puzzle, or played a round of golf better than ever.

2. *Reconstruct this peak performance experience by recalling a physical sensation.* Perhaps you felt a sensation of smoothness and rhythm while swimming, a cool breeze against your cheek and a surge of energy while skiing, lightheartedness while envisioning a new meaning of "freedom," or total absorption and a sense of control during a round of golf.

3. *Recall emotional sensations you had during your peak performance experience.* Perhaps you felt exhilarated while swimming or skiing, emotionally warm toward a friend, ecstatic when you wrote a poem, excited when you solved a puzzle, or confident

and in control on the golf course. Fix these emotions in your mind and write down key words and phrases to describe them.

4. *Fix your optimal performance sensation in your mind and write down key words or phrases to describe it.* You will use these words and phrases later.

Once you have created your phrases, your next step is to use them in combination with the relaxation phrases. Here's a sample set of relaxation phrases, followed by mobilization phrases—a sequence that outlines the finished program. Repeat each phrase four times.

1. *My right arm is becoming heavy.*

2. *Both my arms are becoming heavy.*

3. *My legs are becoming heavy.*

4. *I am resting.*

After achieving a state of relaxation, shift to the mobilization phase. Repeat each mobilization phrase four times.

1. *I am charged with energy.*

2. *I feel tingly.*

3. *My energy seeks expression.*

4. *I act with confidence.*

Take Action

Relaxation and mobilization systems are equally important. Relaxation lays the foundation by helping you clear your mind of worries and troubles. Because of the way your autonomic nervous system is wired, you can't feel both stressed and relaxed at the same time. Thus, relaxation tends to clear the mind of negativity, just as clearing the mind of negativity can promote a relaxed outlook. You launch your mobilization phase from a platform of relaxation. Once you are on the mobilization platform, you are ready to launch into action.

Now, let's do it. Go from relaxation to mobilization by phoning that person you need to call for information, by drafting that series of cover letters, or by speaking up confidently during interviews.

Like most worthwhile undertakings, OPT takes time and practice. But once you develop skill in this maximum-performance approach, you can find applications as diverse as writing a poem and lifting weights. You can use the system innovatively to correct laborious irrational thoughts that are easy to come by but frequently challenging to remove, such as viewing yourself as helpless unless you do everything perfectly. OPT is not about creating perfect performances, because this would be an anxiety-evoking idea. Rather, it's a way to stretch yourself so you can perform better when you need to excel. Once you've mastered this technique, you can use this approach to prepare for situations that require a high degree of focus and optimal performance.

STRATEGIES FOR SUCCESS

Now it's time for you to put these thoughts into action.

KEY IDEAS

1.

2.

3.

ACTION PLAN

1.

2.

3.

IMPLEMENTATION

1.

2.

3.

RESULTS

1.

2.

3.

POSTSCRIPT

No one we know operates at peak performance levels all the time. Your typical performance level will be a little lower. But from time to time, maximum performance is important for achieving a goal. A surprise job interview for a top organization may be such an occasion. When you have limited time to prepare, your power of passionate pursuit and the results of optimal performance training can energize and motivate you to perform at your best when such performances are required to produce a specific desired result.

4 BUILD A PRODUCTIVE JOB-SEARCH ENVIRONMENT

If you are already employed but ready for a new job, we'll share ideas for advancing your search. If you are out of work and searching, it will likely be a full-time job finding work. We'll tell you how to create a job-search environment that applies to either situation.

CREATE A POSITIVE JOB-SEARCH ENVIRONMENT

While you can't control the job market, what work comes onto the market, and whether you'll be invited for an interview, you can control your personal working environment for producing job-search products and for launching initiatives.

When you create a working environment that supports your job-search efforts, you position yourself for success. Here are some basic considerations:

> In this era of the home office, set up a home office environment that promotes your job-search process *before* starting

your search. Your office can even be a corner of a multiuse room, but set it up for minimal distractions.

➤ A productive job-search environment is organized and includes the equipment necessary for you to complete your search as efficiently as possible. If you have a fax machine, a computer with a word-processing program, and a letter-quality ink-jet or laser printer, you have useful tools to do many job-hunting tasks at home. If not, consider acquiring these tools. Because of the growing trend toward e-mail submissions, your most valuable tools may be a computer and Internet access.

➤ Decide what resources you need to help your search process—anything from a computer, transportation, special paper for letters and résumés, and ink cartridges to knowledgeable contacts.

➤ Surround yourself with conditions that inspire action. What search atmosphere can you create that prompts purposeful and productive actions? Is it one where you have an inspiring painting or poster on the wall, where you have Mozart's music playing softly in the background, where your materials are properly filed? Do you have ABCDE forms (see chapter 2) available so you can organize your thinking and reduce needless stress?

➤ Reduce or eliminate distractions from your job-search environment. For example, do you gravitate toward the television set during job-search hours? Are you likely to spend too much time phoning friends to fill the time? Are you working in an environment that you associate with sleep and where you routinely fall asleep (such as your bedroom)?

➤ Avoid "busy work," such as shuffling and reshuffling papers, rereading the newspaper, or washing and polishing the car during business hours. Because busy work creates the illusion of productivity, a professional observer might not notice some busy work. For example, in Connie Wanberg and colleagues' long-term study (see chapter 1), the authors listed some common activities of job searchers. We smile as we note that the researchers found that reading job ads in the newspaper and on the Internet consumed the most time, compared to normally more productive actions like networking, sending out résumés, and contacting employers (Wanberg et al. 2005). Seeking work by reading newspaper ads is busy work, because it's among the least productive methods for finding a job. Eliminating distractions and spending less time on less-productive activities make more time available for more-productive actions.

➤ Reduce or eliminate catalysts for negative thinking. What's in your search environment that's likely to trigger a chain of negative associations? Is your search environment cluttered, souring your aesthetic sense? Do you have pictures of stern-looking relatives on your wall that prompt you to feel guilty for wasting a second of time (feeling guilty wastes more time)?

As an extra benefit of following these suggestions, you put yourself into a favorable position if you wind up getting work you can do from your own home office.

Use the Telephone and E-Mail Effectively

The telephone is one of your most important tools. Use it to call prospective employers, and add call-waiting or call forwarding to your phone service if you don't already have it, to ensure that you don't miss calls. Here are some additional suggestions:

➤ Use voice mail or an answering machine that allows you to retrieve messages and respond to them promptly.

➤ Keep your voice-mail or answering-machine greeting brief, upbeat, and professional—for example, "Hello, this is John Doe. I'm sorry I can't take your call right now, but I look forward to returning your call promptly. Please leave your name and phone number at the sound of the beep. Thank you for calling."

> ➤ Avoid "cute" messages, such as "You have reached Jane Doe and her wonder dog Barney. At the sound of the woof, bark your message." This may attract positive attention in your personal life, but if a prospective interviewer has a dog phobia, you're off on the wrong foot.

> ➤ Carry your cell phone with you and make sure it's charged. Check hourly for messages.

Some employers prefer to communicate by e-mail. Plan to check your e-mail on an hourly basis.

Most e-mail servers have spell-checkers, and some check grammar as well. Use these features to reduce the risk of typos and grammatical errors.

Keep Procrastination Out of Your Home Office

While operating from your home office, you will not only be subject to distractions but also have the flexibility to indulge them. You don't need to keep your nose to the grindstone and clutch every second as if it were your last; that time-stickler attitude is ordinarily unrealistic and probably stressful. On the other hand, it's wise to be mindful of distractions that could significantly detour your job-search mission, because you want to avoid developing self-defeating habits.

For example, you want to set up your home office to maximize efficiency, so you decide to get a new desk with room for all your office equipment. You go from store to store but can't find the "right" desk and then continue looking online to see if you can find it. Feeling stressed searching for a desk, you decide to reward yourself by watching your favorite TV show; you'll renew your desk search tomorrow. When tomorrow comes, you find a potential desk but balk at the price, so you set off on another mission, to find the same desk at a lower price. Meanwhile, you decide to upgrade your fax machine, so you go on that search next.

QUICK TIPS

➤ Finding work takes work, so roll up your sleeves.

➤ Keep your spirits up with such life enhancements as making sure you have a clean automobile (just don't wash it during business hours), having special lunches, or organizing your work area.

➤ Keep in shape by exercising daily for at least a half hour. Exercise adds to your mental alertness, ability to concentrate, and productivity. When you are in good physical shape, you're also more likely to accomplish more with greater confidence, plus you'll project a better physical image.

➤ Receiving sufficient sleep is restorative and helps develop your well-being. If you have bouts of insomnia the first few nights after losing your job and find yourself worrying, you may benefit from leaving your bedroom in the middle of the night and worrying elsewhere. That way, you won't be as likely to associate negative thinking with your bedroom, and your bedroom won't serve as a cue for such thinking (see Knaus 2006 for thirty cognitive, emotive, and behavioral sleep tips).

➤ If there's one piece of advice practically everyone agrees on, it's this: when you are unemployed, getting work is your new full-time job. Prepare yourself to spend at least forty hours a week completing tasks you have identified as necessary for your job search, including looking for new job openings.

➤ Approaching your preparatory job-search tasks with as much zeal as you would if you were doing your "pet" project will boost your odds of getting a position you'll like better than the one you had.

After deciding to compile information for your résumé, you start by looking for an old résumé. It's not in the right file, so you keep going over the same territory looking for it. In the process, you find documents from former jobs and decide to look through them to get inspiration for your new résumé. After many hours of looking at old documents, you feel fatigued and take a nap. When you wake up, you feel uninspired and leave to watch a baseball game.

If you find yourself in a procrastination trap, use the following matrix approach to help you focus on what's most important to do and to avoid distractions. (For an in-depth approach to breaking through procrastination barriers and staying on track with your job search, see Knaus, in press.) Here's how: in the following chart, your priority is the top item in the "Timely" box. Among the many things you do, your job search will likely be your most timely and important activity. Though finding a new desk may be useful, it isn't pressing. Reading old files may not be that important either.

PRIORITY MATRIX

ACTION	Important	Useful	Unimportant
Timely			
Not pressing			

If, in the course of conducting your job search, you find that you emphasize less pressing and less important activities, the odds are that these activities are procrastination diversions. You now have an opportunity to revisit your self-observant approach and guide your "horse" (see chapter 3) in the direction of productivity.

Manage Your Time Efficiently

"Time-management training" is often a euphemism for getting people to work harder in organizations, which gives the phrase the reputation of a tax audit. But when you are on a job search, how you manage your time can influence the quality and outcome of your search. For example, you will normally do better when you keep an active pace and put good-faith efforts into meeting your job-search priorities.

You can go overboard with time management by getting stuck in the time stickler trap, which is when you get uptight about losing time and lose even more time complaining about lost time.

We've seen job searchers straitjacket themselves by overscheduling. If you create a schedule so demanding that the Roman god Mercury couldn't move fast enough to stick to it, this will deepen any discouragement you feel.

Estimating the time it takes to finish certain job-search tasks can be a challenging undertaking. The best you can do is make a rough estimate, and how you pace yourself can make a difference. If you operate at a typical pace, you can still streamline your actions by avoiding distractions. You'll likely follow a bits-and-pieces approach, where you work step by step at your more timely and important priorities, then go on to the ones the next level down.

Certain activities will require your maximum and speediest efforts. For example, if you receive a job interview scheduled for tomorrow afternoon at two o'clock, you'll have to step up your efforts to prepare.

Planned periods of downtime can improve your job-search productivity. Within your forty hours of job-search time, you have reasonable flexibility. For example, most organizations assume you'll put in about thirty-two hours a week in actual job performance, so they adjust salaries accordingly.

If you treat your job search like a full-time job, then after deducting eight hours for sleep each night you have seventy-two hours a week left over for doing whatever you want to do. You are likely to do better than average by working forty hours a week on your job search. Stepping up the pace by putting in some "overtime" will further tip the chances in your favor, but know your limits.

DROP TIME HOGS

What's your typical pace? Can you find ways to operate at your typical pace and still cut out nonessential activities? Cutting out time hogs can help you make more efficient use of your job-search time.

A *time hog* is an unessential or low-priority activity that consumes far more time than it's worth. Some extreme examples are spending an hour daily scrubbing your bathroom or washing and rewashing your car, or taking an hour on the phone to convey a two-minute message. But less-obvious time hogs can slip under the radar, such as reading and rereading past e-mail messages you've sent, or daydreaming.

How do you achieve a balance between job-search activities and the normal activities of daily life? The answer is simple: keep your priorities straight. Doing so typically involves preparing to meet such challenges and then doing whatever it takes to maintain balance.

Part of establishing a balance involves establishing a do-it-now philosophy. During your job-search hours, conduct your search in a reasonable way within a reasonable time to achieve your objectives. Your relationships, hobbies, and downtime are also part of the do-it-now way. In your off-hours, relax and recreate. If you golf or socialize on the weekends, continue doing these activities. Using downtime well can help you maintain a positive momentum in your job search.

YOUR WORK STYLE: BY SCHEDULE OR BY PROJECT

When your full-time job is finding a job, how you organize your time and resources is a matter of personal preference. It's *your* job search; it's your opportunity to stay in tune with what you do when you work effectively.

When you're working most effectively, how do you use your resources and time? We've observed that some people are inclined to work better when they follow a reasonable schedule, and others when they work by project, concentrating on one phase of a project and then moving on to another when that phase is completed.

The more concretely you construe a task, the more likely you'll get it done without procrastinating (McCrea et al. 2008). So it's important to be specific about what you'll do during each phase. "I'll learn about résumé writing" differs from "To familiarize myself with writing résumés, I will find three sample résumés and study the design and content of each."

Can you schedule this task between 9:00 and 9:45 a.m., or does it make more sense to put the task on a to-do list, work on it until you've accomplished it, and then cross it off your list?

You may prefer to work on a project-by-project basis, concentrating on one task until you are ready for another. For this method, you may prefer to follow a to-do list. Others prefer to schedule time on an hourly basis. Whatever your solution, pretend your job-search time is worth $350 an hour—how could you best use your time?

You may prefer using a systematic and procedural approach to a broad project approach for the same results. Since this is *your* job search, do it your way. This is rarely an either-or approach; it's one of emphasis. If you don't take the initiative and enter the uncertainty of the job search, you'll stay stuck in place. If you have great ideas and don't create an organized framework for expressing them—including following procedures and time lines—you are likely to fritter away your abilities.

Working by schedule and working by project are complementary strategies for keeping focused on finding your preferred job. You can draw from both approaches.

If you work better by project and intend to emphasize this approach but augment it with a scheduled approach, consider these tactics:

> ➤ Get an appointment book and use it to block out your time commitments. Block out times for locating job openings, reviewing opportunities, sending letters, or making phone contacts.

> ➤ Schedule time for meeting with people who can champion your cause and hook you up with the right hiring authorities.

> ➤ Follow through promptly on phone messages from potential job contacts. Fast follow-through sends a positive message to a prospective employer.

If you work best by schedule, consider these project tactics to augment your current plan:

> ➤ Whenever you undertake a task, stop and ask, "How does this fit with my job-search mission? What's the most effective way to get the task done?"

> ➤ Play the role of an explorer by seeking options through observing, questioning, and investigating.

> ➤ As you decide how to approach an interview, have some ideas for how you will explain what happened at your last job, what you seek, and what you know you can contribute.

Blending schedule and project methods in a proportion that fits your style can put the best of both systems into play. Combined, working by schedule and by project supports the three "P's" of progress that are prominent in the lives of productive people: preparation, persistence, and perspiration.

BOOST YOUR SELF-REGULATION SKILLS

The path to securing a new job depends on many coordinated actions. Each phase of this process has unique features that involve different functions and talents. Through the channels we follow in this process, we find that the means to secure a new job is both complex and simple. It's complex in that there are layers of related activities you normally need to promote and coordinate: making contacts, creating your résumé, writing letters, researching prospective employers, responding effectively to interview questions, and so forth. It's also simple because you direct your activities toward achieving a single goal: securing compensation through employment.

A primary challenge involves effectively harnessing your thoughts to efficiently guide your job-search actions, which requires making an extra effort to direct yourself through a focused and organized course of action that's instrumental to securing a new job. You do this by devising instructions, saying them aloud, then repeating and following them. You might even want to record these instructions on paper and check each phase off when it's completed. Here are sample directives that give you an idea of how this self-instruction support plan works.

> ➤ *For when you have trouble getting started*: "I will identify and then dispute negative thoughts that interfere with mobilizing

my resources to get a job. What am I telling myself right now that causes me to lose ambition and sidetracks my efforts?"

> *For when you first start to write a letter*: "I will begin by booting my computer (or gathering paper and pen). Next I will outline (or sketch) ideas that convey my message. I will pick the thoughts that best fit what I want to say. I will organize these thoughts. I will revise and refine the letter. I will write the name, address, and salutation. I will close and sign off, ask a friend to proofread my letter, and mail it. Now, for step one, I will gather my materials..."

> *For when you develop your résumé*: "I will first gather the tools I want to draft my résumé (such as getting some paper and a pencil, or booting my computer). I will complete the résumé creation guidelines (see chapter 6) so I can organize my information. I will choose a résumé style. I will plug my worksheet data into the style to make an attractive presentation. I will identify an editor to check the material for form and spelling. I will print the finished product."

In each case, the instructions define activities that support your goal of becoming reemployed. Keep your statements brief, express them in the active voice, and identify yourself as the actor.

Monitor Your Progress

Self-monitoring starts with observing how you go about achieving your shorter-term objectives related to your job search. Because the result of getting reemployed is a by-product of what you do to get the job, you want to be sure you stay on the right track.

Use a "Data-Gathering Worksheet" to set an objective for your daily job-search activities. You can jot down your objectives, planned actions, results, and follow-up on a daily schedule. Take a few minutes to use your notebook or computer to devise your own worksheet, like the following example:

DATA-GATHERING WORKSHEET

Objective:				
(*Example:* "Secure ten interviews a month.")				
Schedule:				
Day	*Time*	*Activities*	*Results*	*Follow-up*
Mon				
Tue				
Wed				
Thur				
Fri				
Sat				
Sun				

At the end of each week, use the following summary sheet to summarize how you used your time in high-priority job-search activities compared to low-priority activities. Use this information to monitor your efforts, to progress, and to make adjustments:

SUMMARY SHEET

High-Priority Activities	**Time Spent**	**Results**
1.		
2.		
3.		
4.		
5.		

Low-Priority Activities	Time Spent	Results
1.		
2.		
3.		
4.		
5.		

Under "High-Priority Activities," you might discover that you made five networking calls a day, sent five follow-up letters a day, and revised your résumé to make it mesh with a special job opportunity. Under "Low-Priority Activities," you might notice a habit of drinking coffee and reading the newspaper between 8:00 and 10:00 a.m. Then you watch the stock-market ticker tape on TV until about noon, followed by lunch. Next you make your calls and send out your letters. If you find that you engage in more than eight hours of unimportant and nonpressing activities during your weekly job-search schedule, you can take corrective steps sooner rather than later. This information rolls over to ways of improving your efficiency and effectiveness.

Efficiency-Boosting Measures

Self-monitoring is a sensible way to focus on your search and to reduce or eliminate activities that get in the way. The following activity helps you decrease time spent doing unimportant and nonpressing activities and increase time spent on higher-order ones.

Activities to Increase	Activities to Decrease
Example: Sending résumé and cover letter to at least five firms a day	*Example:* Reading the newspaper from 8:00 to 10:00 a.m.

SELF-REINFORCEMENT

Many of life's rewards are subtle, only becoming obvious when we consider the consequences of not having them. For example, when you stop at a stop sign, you reward yourself by avoiding an accident. Such rewards raise the frequency of a response.

Rewards might either hinder or help a job-search effort. They hinder when they reinforce avoidance activities. When drinking coffee, phoning friends, or reading a novel gets in the way of purposeful job-search activities, this avoidance behavior promotes temporary relief, which reinforces avoidance. We may avoid some job opportunities because we don't feel worthy enough to pursue the challenge. Nevertheless, many of us dodge temporarily frustrating situations every day because we don't want to feel discomfort.

You can turn some avoidance rewards into true rewards for your job-search actions. If you find that you too often divert yourself from job-search activities by drinking coffee and reading the newspaper before you start your search activities, reverse the process. By restructuring your schedule, you can use these diversions to advantage. Instead, start with your job-search efforts, and follow these efforts with the pleasurable activities. Allow yourself, say, twenty minutes to read the paper and drink a cup of coffee after every hour and a half of search activities. By arranging a schedule of rewards so that the reward follows a *desired action*, you get a double positive. The reward will increase the frequency of the response it follows, plus it feels good.

What rewards will work for you? Your perceptions, situation, values, knowledge, priorities, and life direction will influence your choice of reward. Eating an apple, going to a movie, and reading a newspaper all are viable rewards, provided they raise your frequency of purposeful behavior.

Dispensing rewards requires a disciplined approach. We can all "cheat" on dispensing a reward to ourselves by dropping the standard or by taking the reward in advance. The system works best when rewards are self-administered and consistent with the plan.

You don't have to dispense the reward if the conditions aren't ripe. For example, writing letters and making calls can repeatedly remind you of your job loss, which may bring an undercurrent of depression. So, if you feel depressed after a few hours of writing cover letters, this is not the time to reward yourself with an ice-cream cone. Instead, use REBT methods (see chapter 2) to challenge the thoughts accompanying your depressed mood. When you have shrunk the impact of your depressing ideas, the relief you feel can be a suitable reward.

STRATEGIES FOR SUCCESS

Setting up a functional and workable career-search environment is an important preliminary effort. When you have your resources at your fingertips, you are better organized and can operate more efficiently, sparing yourself the frustrations and aggravations of a chaotic job search. Take time to determine what you will do to build a job-search environment that boosts your efficiency and effectiveness.

KEY IDEAS

1.

2.

3.

ACTION PLAN

1.

2.

3.

IMPLEMENTATION

1.

2.

3.

RESULTS

1.

2.

3.

POSTSCRIPT

In chapter 3 you explored answering four questions to define your purposeful passion. In this chapter, the distinction between working by schedule and by project added another dimension to matching your interests, purpose, and attributes to a career and to advancing your passionate purpose. In chapter 5 we'll go into greater depth on how to develop your career profile.

PART 2

GET ROLLING ON
A SUCCESSFUL JOB
SEARCH

5 CREATE YOUR CAREER PROFILE

This is a book on how to get a great job, not on selecting a career direction, yet it's hard to separate the two. Seeking a match between your strengths and interests and your employment is a big step in the direction of earning a living and making your contribution to the world with a sense of accomplishment and fulfillment. It doesn't make sense to find a "great job" without considering what would actually be a great job for you.

It's rare when someone sticks throughout a lifetime with a career choice made in childhood. You are likely to make multiple career choices and changes over a life span, whether prompted by changes in the economy, different stages of life, your life conditions, or your career and educational accomplishments. As changes take place around you, it's important to know yourself as well as what work functions you can competently perform and learn. Then you can transfer this knowledge and these skills to emerging opportunities. It's also important to know how your skills and characteristics fit those of people who are enjoying success in their careers. Master carpenters have more in common with each other than with theoretical physicists. Attorneys have more in common with each other than they do with physicians or paper-mill machinists.

In this chapter we'll share some basic ideas about how to explore different career directions, including how to connect your career values, interests, and skills to get on a satisfying career track. We'll also suggest how to avoid excessively stressful work. Another reason to get to know yourself in deciding a career direction is that it helps you craft your résumé and cover letters. Also, when you apply for work you feel genuinely enthusiastic about because it fits what you want to do and can do, your enthusiasm will resonate positively in an interview as much as your qualifications will.

JOB CONGRUENCE AND WORK SATISFACTION

Though we know of no fail-safe way to find an ideal job, the more you know yourself and your skills, work values, and work preferences, the closer you are to deciding whether a job or career direction is more or less right for you.

The closer you can come to getting paid for what you like to do, the closer you'll get to congruence among what you know about yourself, what you prefer to do for work, and the work you actually do (Holland 1996).

Johns Hopkins professor and career specialist John Holland (ibid.) regards everyone as fitting into one or more career types:

➤ *Realistic*: Practical, physical, hands-on, tool-oriented

➤ *Investigative*: Analytical, intellectual, scientific, tending to explore

➤ *Artistic*: Creative, original, independent, chaotic

➤ *Social*: Cooperative, supportive, helpful, healing or nurturing

➤ *Enterprising*: Preferring competitive environments, leadership-oriented, persuasive

➤ *Conventional*: Detail-oriented, organized, clerical

You can rank these work preferences from high to low and match your higher preferences to job descriptions. For example, if your two top areas are social and realistic, you may find greater satisfaction teaching in a technological field or working as a physical therapist than managing a retail store. Studying your personality in relation to these types will likely sharpen your career options and improve your career decisions (Tracey 2008). Congruence favorably affects job satisfaction and work performance (Tracey and Robbins 2006; Tsabari, Tziner, and Meir 2005). The bottom line is that it's definitely desirable to find a good fit between your interests and talents and the job you do.

Job stress is common in any work setting. It's how you handle stress that makes the difference. For example, in its day, Louis "Studs" Terkel's (1972) book *Working* was popular among career counselors and general readers. If you plow through Terkel's 589-page tome, you'll see that few people described finding joy through their work.

Although work stress may result from a mismatch between the person and the job, it's more often the result of unnecessarily magnified negative thinking about a situation. Whatever the cause, work stress is the source of about 40 percent of workplace turnover and about 80 percent of all work-related injuries (Atkinson 2004).

Cognitive behavioral therapy, an offshoot of REBT and behavioral therapy, is an effective approach for reducing job stress (Richardson and Rothstein 2008). However, if your biggest source of stress is other people's behavior, the REBT method for keeping things in perspective applies to reducing such stress. Along with early career guidance programs for elementary and junior-high students (Ganley and Elias 1966), learning to apply the REBT method to manage stress can open opportunities for greater job satisfaction and higher productivity.

YOUR CAREER DECISION CENTER

The U.S. Department of Labor's *Dictionary of Occupational Titles* (1991) contains over twelve thousand primary job titles, from abalone diver to zoo veterinarian. Variations on the primary job themes bring the number of titles to over twenty-eight thousand, so it's unlikely you'll be stumped for long about career possibilities. You can also find updated occupational titles on O*NET OnLine (online.onetcenter.org), a federally supported website with information on job descriptions, moving into a related career, developing a résumé, and more.

If you are thinking about making a career change or want to ascertain the future for your current career, the latest U.S. Department of Labor *Occupational Outlook Handbook* (in press) contains descriptions of work functions, training and educational requirements, future work opportunities, and range of salary across all major occupational groups. (Most libraries own hard copies of this reference, but you can also find it at online.onetcenter.org.) So, there's a job out there for you, and there are probably many different career tracks that fit your talents, interests, and experiences.

If you are like most people, you want to find a fit between what you are good at and what the job requires. Being in a field that's right for you and for the most part doing what you like to do would qualify as a great job.

How important is finding a positive career direction? Can't you be trained for a career of any type? That type of hit-or-miss method is more likely to miss than hit. A random career selection amounting to throwing a dart at a career list violates much of what psychologists know about individual differences. We think career assessment is an area worth exploring.

A careful career analysis can confirm your current career direction, suggest a variation, or point in a promising new direction. The greater value of this assessment lies in your thinking out what's best for you to do or confirming what you already believe to be true.

To support your career assessment progress, create a *career decision center* for yourself. This is your psychological warehouse of information about careers that appeal to you. You can make the center part of your job-search home office, but it represents more of a process than a specific location, meaning that the center can be any place where you can store and analyze career information.

Quick Tips

➤ If applicable to your situation, use the *Dictionary of Occupational Titles* to learn about a large variety of potential jobs.

➤ Make an inventory of your aptitudes, abilities, and interests by jotting down things you know about yourself related to your work skills and interests.

➤ Do your own assessment of SWTLO (strengths, weaknesses, threats, limitations, and opportunities; introduced in the next section).

➤ Match your abilities with specific job functions to determine your ideal job.

A KNOW-YOURSELF APPROACH TO CAREER CHOICE

Making a personal career competencies profile is an important step to putting yourself on the path to greater work satisfaction and success. Take the following steps to develop your career profile:

1. Assess your academic, personal, and work abilities; aptitudes; and accomplishments.

2. Analyze your strengths, weaknesses, threats, limitations, and opportunities (SWTLO).

3. Identify the functions associated with your ideal job.

4. Identify skills that can earn you the most money in the least amount of time.

5. Take standardized interest, aptitude, and abilities tests.

Though each dimension will overlap with the others to some extent, it will also provide unique information. Your challenge is to complete the exercises and integrate the applicable information into your career planning.

Assess Your Abilities, Aptitudes, and Accomplishments

Work aptitudes accompany work interests because most of us like to do what we feel accomplished at doing. To generate this information, start listing the following:

1. In what school subjects did you get your best grades (physical sciences, mathematics, history, human sciences, English, foreign languages, and so on)?

2. What extracurricular activities did you seek out because you were good at doing them (academic clubs, sports, arts, debate, advocacy, and so on)?

3. What hobbies and special interests overlap your career direction (organizing outings; coaching Little League; collecting, organizing, and recording information about rare coins; persuading and debating; fixing and repairing; researching; designing and planning gardens; playing golf, planning parties, participating in community activities)?

4. In your performance reviews, which of your qualities did your supervisors list as strengths?

5. What career awards or accomplishments can you cite?

Now summarize your list of interests and accomplishments:

YOUR INTERESTS AND ACCOMPLISHMENTS

Dimension	Examples
1. School subjects	
2. Extracurricular activities	
3. Hobbies	
4. Performance review	
5. Career awards	

Your SWTLO Analysis

Now use the previous information for your SWTLO analysis. As mentioned, SWTLO stands for strengths, weaknesses, threats, limitations, and opportunities. This model is a useful way to organize your career information.

In your SWTLO analysis, your strengths and weaknesses are all relative to your other personal attributes. For example, are you better at writing than speaking? Are you better at analyzing than creating? Are you better at delegating than doing tasks yourself? For your SWTLO assessment, answer the following questions:

1. *What are your strengths, talents, and capabilities (what you do well)?* Do you have a broad range of experience you can apply in response to changes in the job market? Do you have accounting skills? Do you have negotiating skills? Do you have effective communication skills, including active listening, reading, writing, and public speaking? Are you an effective teacher? Can you design, make, fix, or build devices? Can you solve mechanical problems? Can you design methods to improve production? Can you envision, create, invent, or generate opportunities? Do you manage time effectively? Do you have a high frustration tolerance? Do you have an amiable nature? Do you have a curious mind? Do you have teaching skills? Do you delegate effectively? Are you a skilled planner and organizer? Can you persuade, inspire, sell, and motivate? Are you an objective observer who can investigate, research, collect information, analyze data, find trends, and decide courses of action?

2. *List your work faults or weaknesses—we all have them!* Do you attend too much to detail? Do you find it difficult to end business calls? Are you slow to respond to personnel problems, such as employee lateness? Do you too often overlook office politics? Do you take on too many responsibilities? Do you make your decisions based on "gut impressions" before reviewing the facts? Do you delegate too much or too little? Are you slow to follow up? Do you react to problems rather than prevent them? Do you slide over ideas unless they fit with your own interests?

3. *What do you consider to be your most significant career threats?* Are you behind in the technology and knowledge of your field? Do you need to develop your computer skills? Is your specialty becoming obsolete? Do you feel as if you are slowing down or losing enthusiasm for what you do?

4. *What conditions limit your career opportunities and choices?* Did you learn a specialized proprietary control system for your previous employer that won't readily transfer to another company? Do you lack a college degree in an area that normally requires a higher education? Do you hold an advanced degree but prefer work that doesn't require one? Are you an expert in a specialty market that typically provides few job opportunities?

5. *What are your career opportunities?* Do you want to switch careers? Do you want to get into your own business? Do you want to buy into a successful franchise? Do you want to leap-frog to a higher position than the one you left? Do you want to move to a "dream region" of the country? Do you want to add to your education and obtain a degree to support your advancement interests? Do you have a highly specialized skill that you can sell as a consultant? Do you want to work for an organization where you have considerable autonomy? Do you want a position that involves frequent travel? Do you want to have a shorter commute? Do you want a position where you can gain recognition for your accomplishments?

Here's an abbreviated sample of an SWTLO assessment:

Sample SWTLO Assessment

Strengths: Intelligent, have sense of humor, am socially cordial, have strong character
Weaknesses: Sometimes have difficulty backing away from a position, get easily sidetracked
Threats: My current skill set may be rendered obsolete by new technology
Limitations: Education, range of experience
Opportunities: Job retraining based on compatibility among skill sets, interests, and aptitudes

Now it's your turn to complete your SWTLO assessment:

YOUR SWTLO ASSESSMENT

Strengths:
Weaknesses:
Threats:
Limitations:
Opportunities:

Define Your Ideal Job

What career activities do you prefer to do—for example, gather information, analyze, plan, organize, monitor or control, communicate, solve customer problems, measure financial results, manage a marketing department, or sell? Mapping out your preferences gives you three advantages: you (1) clarify the type of meaningful work you want to accomplish, (2) match the results of your analysis against a potential job opportunity, and (3) have a profile to match against a job description. Independent of the job title, the third advantage adds a means to match your preferred job functions with your job responsibilities.

In developing your profile, consider these five career-preference dimensions:

1. *What do you consider to be purposeful and productive work?* People who work at jobs they view as purposeful and productive experience a sense of fulfillment and have an abundance of career satisfaction. Start with your most recent job and work back to your school graduation. What work efforts gave you the most satisfaction? Then group these functions into general categories like helping people, solving problems, or following through.

2. *What are your preferred work functions?* Work involves different tasks, some of which we enjoy and others of which we find unpleasant, even stressful. People who find satisfaction in their work have more job duties they find enjoyable. Job activities include a broad spectrum, such as writing a report, making a sales call, tilling a field, researching a problem, or devising a plan. List the work functions you enjoyed most on the job. Did you enjoy making plans? Did your most enjoyable job functions relate to organizing, training, selling, or troubleshooting?

3. *What are your primary work values?* Do you persist until you finish? Do you value making quality products? Do you value conscientiousness? Do you value loyalty? Do you see yourself as acting responsibly even at a personal cost?

4. *What are your primary work dispositions and qualities?* It's useful to consider career directions that fit your disposition. If you are energetic and competitive, you may feel stressed working at a job that requires you to behave deferentially. If you have a sensitive temperament, you may experience stress while working in an environment where you have to deal with aggressive people. If you prefer to work by yourself, you may feel stressed if your job requires you to primarily work with and through others. Do you prefer working with people or with things? Do you like technical work or working with ideas? Do you like being creative and innovative, or do you prefer to add to ideas or plans that have already been generated? What type of environment do you prefer: indoors or outdoors, the city or the country?

5. *At what occupational level do you operate most effectively?* When you test your abilities, you discover how far you can stretch. Nevertheless, knowing your limitations provides a different perspective in defining your career track. The exceptional salesperson may flounder as a sales manager, because each role requires different functions. Still, if you don't stretch far enough, you will have fewer accomplishments and will probably feel frustrated.

Following is a sample career-preference profile:

SAMPLE CAREER-PREFERENCE PROFILE

What do you consider to be purposeful work? A professional career that involves variety, change, and opportunities to learn and contribute
What are your preferred job functions? Helping people resolve their personal problems, training others to develop their skills, meeting complex challenges, creating innovative approaches to solving problems, bringing people together for a common purpose, developing strategies for change, dealing with crises
What are your primary work values? Working with people with high energy and integrity who feel committed to what they do; producing quality products that improve people's lives
What are your primary work dispositions and qualities? Willingness to persist and persevere, stable, empathic, able to deal with conflict effectively, reasonable, honest, creative, direct and assertive, willing to take risks and learn
At what occupational level do you operate most effectively? Executive-level responsibilities

Now, it's your turn to develop your career-preference profile:

YOUR CAREER-PREFERENCE PROFILE

What do you consider to be purposeful work?
What are your preferred job functions?
What are your primary work values?
What are your primary work dispositions and qualities?
At what occupational level do you operate most effectively?

The career-preference profile has additional value: if an interviewer asks you how you see yourself fit into the job, you can specifically match what you know about yourself to what you know about the position.

Rapid Money-Producing Skills

The primary reason to work is for money. You will be most efficient at earning money when you concentrate on what's profitable, focus on a field in which you have talent, and work hard at what comes easiest. This is the secret of the rapid-fire money producers. Members of this unique group earn money in proportion to the value other people place on their skills, and also in proportion to their talents in their chosen work. They include top entertainers, competent managers, and world-class athletes.

To think like a rapid money producer, ask yourself, "How can I make the most money in the most enjoyable way?" Consider these questions:

> What resources do you have that could make you the most income?

> What's the market for using these skills and talents?

> What's the entry fee? For example, do you need a college degree, or is there a specific skill you need that would require special training and cost time and money to obtain?

> Are you willing to pay the price?

> What can you expect in return for your efforts?

Some of this information is useful when you are considering switching careers or making better use of your talents in your present career.

Use Standardized Career Inventories

There are a number of helpful standardized career tests and inventories you can use to help you identify careers that would be a good fit. A career counseling center or a licensed vocational psychologist can administer these instruments. A basic career inventory battery may include a measure of interest (such as the Strong Interest Inventory), a measure of temperament (Sixteen Personality Factor Questionnaire, or 16PF), and a measure of style (Myers-Briggs Type Indicator). Licensed and qualified vocational professionals use the Strong Interest Inventory and 16PF measures. A vocational psychologist will also have access to a broad range of aptitude test measures to give you information about your strongest aptitudes, such as mechanical, selling, or clerical ability.

Standardized aptitude measures can save time and effort by pointing you in the direction of areas to explore. Tempering them with reality checks adds to their value. For example, you may have interest patterns in common with musicians, a compatible temperament, and a social style that fits a general musician profile. But if you are also tone deaf, performing is probably not for you. Even so, you may also have the interest, temperament, and style of a talent agent. Maybe your profile predicts that you have much in common with your musician clients, and this type of rapport can provide enjoyment as well as advantages in this line of work.

You may have much in common with lawyers and have many lawyer friends. However, at the age of fifty-five, getting a law degree and passing the bar examination may be impractical. Yet you may find options you hadn't considered, and that information can have special value if you are considering a career change.

Reliable and valid career measures have a significant advantage over homegrown measures peddled by unlicensed people who claim to be experts without going through the academic rigors and don't meet professional licensing standards. Many of these self-appointed "experts" aren't aware of what they don't know, nor is there any science behind the products they peddle. Standardized measures have scientific support. As the saying goes, "*Caveat emptor*," or "Let the buyer beware."

CAREER-CHANGE CHALLENGES

The reasons people change careers include promotions, obsolete skills, burnout, the opportunity to do something desired and different, new insights into career interests and values, the need for more satisfaction, and escape from a bad situation.

If your current career requires you to do functions that largely fall into your "weaknesses" column, you may want to consider other opportunities that are more compatible with your strengths, interests, and temperament. This will mean considering a job that allows you to transfer some of your strengths and preferred functions while providing an occasion to start tracking in a direction that's consistent with your long-term goals. If you find that you are on the right track, then the issue is finding the best available opportunities and taking initiative to get the best job.

In your career profile, you defined purposeful work for yourself, the work functions you prefer, your strongest abilities, your work values, your dispositions, and the work level that most closely fits your skills and capabilities. This provides criteria to compare to a job description. If the description calls for performing many of your preferred functions, you may have found a great opportunity. Selling yourself, however, presents another challenge.

In considering a new career, how do you put together the information you gathered? If you are a visionary thinker with sound technical skills, perhaps you might function more happily and effectively in an entrepreneurial organization. If you prefer to apply experience to new situations, then a larger organization that follows sound operating policies and procedures may be to your liking. If you have a good imagination and talent in writing, and you like to work alone, perhaps you could write a newspaper column or a company newsletter.

It pays to remember that with over twenty-eight thousand different occupations, it's virtually impossible to love all career possibilities or to find that you don't fit any option. The ancient Greeks had the right idea with the phrase "Know thyself." But we go one step further: know yourself *and* your options. Use this information to decide on a direction, and follow through on your decision without procrastinating.

Your career assessment may suggest that getting specialized education is in your long-term best interest. In down economic cycles, when jobs are hard to come by, if you have the resources to start a college or specialty training program, and can enter the workforce as the economy takes an upturn, you will have taken advantage of an economic lull while positioning yourself for future career growth.

STRATEGIES FOR SUCCESS

You may have known the work you wanted to do since you were a child, but if you are like most people, such certainty comes through a funneling-down process that takes place over many years, after many experiences. You may still have room in your funnel to refine and sharpen your career direction. If so, you will open up opportunities to move toward the satisfaction that comes from doing enjoyable and productive work. Completing the following activities can set you in a productive job-search direction.

KEY IDEAS

1.

2.

3.

ACTION STEPS

1.

2.

3.

IMPLEMENTATION

1.

2.

3.

RESULTS

1.

2.

3.

POSTSCRIPT

Imagine the potential benefits of knowing yourself and how your skills fit a career direction in which you have interest and talent. In that work environment, you are likely to display a positive attitude and productive work performance. That's a win-win situation for you and your future employer.

6 LOOK GOOD ON PAPER

Your cover letter and résumé are likely the first documents a gatekeeper will see. Since most screeners have a short attention span, your cover letter and résumé will be quickly read. Making a positive first, quick impression gives you the opportunity to make a great second impression.

Your résumé is essential for getting your foot in the door. You can easily find numerous examples of résumés, including models for conveying résumé information in a letter and for formatting résumés for e-mail and online submission. We'll describe two traditional forms: chronological and functional. In creating your résumé, you'll have limited space to lay out your credentials. Keep the appearance of your résumé clean and uncluttered. What you put down on your résumé will surely be a topic during the interview phase of your job search. Avoid being shy about your accomplishments, but also pick the most relevant information and keep it factual. If you are a serious candidate for a position, most responsible organizations will check the facts.

A one-page résumé formatted in a conservative style tends to get the best response. But if you use a two-page résumé, put the key information about your job-relevant experience and education up front. There are, of course, exceptions to using a traditional style. For example, if you are applying for a graphic-artist position, you may want to use a different font and formatting style than if you applied for a supervisory position.

Regardless of what résumé style and format you follow, you need to include two core pieces of content employers look for: your educational credentials and related work experience. Make this information prominent.

This chapter will show you how to develop high-impact résumés and cover letters for both traditional and online presentation. Then you'll see how to set up your résumé for electronic submission. You'll learn how to use networking websites to get the word out about your availability and credentials. Later, you'll find a sample cover letter for introducing yourself to a gatekeeper or decision maker.

GATHER MATERIALS FOR YOUR RÉSUMÉ

Creating an attractive résumé is a matter of putting job-relevant content into a concise format, but doing so is typically a work in process until you say what you want, the way you want—and know that you're saying it effectively. Plan to edit your efforts multiple times.

Here are three quick-start guidelines:

1. Start with a statement describing the title of the position you want. This can be anything from supervising engineer for a medium-sized polymer plant to customer service representative for an automotive products company to chief executive officer of a Fortune 500 company to laborer for a paving company.

2. Create a list of your preferred responsibilities, including tasks you feel qualified to accomplish, such as organizing, speaking, coordinating, managing, team building, analyzing data, developing spreadsheets, detailing, selling—anything that represents a paid function you are good at.

3. Define a series of purposeful actions to achieve your desired result, including writing or updating your résumé; deciding where and how you will look for work; writing generic cover letters; preparing answers to common interview questions; and seeking work opportunities through networking, search firms, advertisements, and telephone and mail inquiries.

QUICK TIPS

➤ Begin by thinking about your objective. Use information from your work in chapter 5 to define your objective.

➤ Organize your job history into a pithy and attention-grabbing format, showing dates and important job functions you've performed.

➤ Highlight your strongest skills and the job functions you'd especially like to perform, but avoid creating the appearance that these are the only things you want to do. Most jobs have responsibilities that aren't popular or pleasant, and your willingness to accept those responsibilities can give you an edge.

➤ Review résumé formats to see which style you think will work best for you as well as what style will likely have the best impact on employers. You are crafting the résumé for employers, not for what pleases you the most.

➤ Screeners will likely look for these three things first: Do you have the job experience? Do you have the educational background? Are there red flags that would disqualify you? Get a knowledgeable person's feedback about your résumé.

➤ Keep your information accurate. If you appear to walk on water, you may raise a red flag. But underplaying your credentials, which is a common error, may cause you to be overlooked.

➤ Consider using your résumé to expand your job search by posting your credentials through electronic job resources: résumé-posting sites, job-vacancy databases, employer websites, or other career information sites.

Developing a smart résumé usually takes planning and reworking. If writing isn't your cup of tea, have someone who's skilled in grammar and spelling review your résumé before you send it out. A misspelled word or other typo may catch the eye of a perfectionistic screener. On the other hand, some screeners may not notice or care, but why take a risk you can eliminate?

Career Objective

A logical place to start is with your career objective and competency statement. Screeners expect to see this first, and one sentence or phrase is usually sufficient—for example, "To create effective software product illustrations for a large computer game company," "To contribute to the productivity of the sales department through my networking and knowledge of the product line," "To provide accurate data and analysis using spreadsheets in the marketing of paper products." Notice that the objective includes doing something to solve a problem and support your future employer's need or mission.

When your résumé is saved as a word-processing file, you can modify your objective to conform it to a job advertisement. That's the beauty of having that flexibility. But when you are clear on your objective (and your work in chapter 5 can help pin that down), you will likely keep your objective true to what you offer and to the job requirement.

A critical point is to avoid citing an objective that's inconsistent with the job. If the position is for a proofreader, an objective to become the chief operating officer in three years will put your résumé right into the "circular file."

Skills and Abilities

You likely can pull together information from chapter 5 to define your skills, including your general skills and abilities used in your hobbies. For example, are you effective at scheduling and keeping appointments for yourself, others, or both? Do you often make to-do lists and check them off as you accomplish various daily tasks? Do you write letters or reports well and easily? Do you communicate persuasively with your peers or supervisors? Are you skilled at breaking down a large job into smaller, doable parts? Jot down skills that aren't necessarily related to one job but could be part of a variety of jobs. It's helpful to note abilities that are broad in scope and can be applied to a variety of positions, as well as those that are more specific to a particular industry or occupation.

Special-Circumstance Issues

If you are in the unfortunate position to have been out of work because of an injury or disability, you face a special challenge. Despite what employers may publicly say about having a nondiscriminatory approach to hiring, some may hesitate to risk hiring someone with workers' compensation or health issues, especially lower-back injuries. Maybe such companies have had legal issues and settlement costs in the past and want to avoid future headaches. So, despite having hard-won protection under the law, you may still find yourself on an uneven playing field.

The majority of employers seek to comply with federal and state regulations regarding hiring qualified applicants, but some do skirt the law, and such job discrimination is unfair. You can find information about your rights as a job applicant at www.doleta.gov/disability, as well as in the Americans with Disabilities Act (available at www.ada.gov/pubs/ada .htm).

We admit it can be challenging to find employment after a worker's compensation claim, when you are over fifty, or when you have a disability, but most organizations just seek people who can do the job.

What are your options? If you have special skills, we suggest emphasizing them on your résumé. Make a special effort to match your skills to a specific job. This is generally a good prescription for all job hunters to follow. Emphasize any job-related education you acquired after the injury or disability. This shows a positive attitude and willingness to take extra steps. Most Americans sympathize with people who make a special effort to improve under conditions of adversity. Research organizations, including governmental agencies, are known for picking people based on their competency.

It's important to convey a positive attitude. The principles you learned in chapter 2 can help you genuinely project a positive attitude and the positive emotions extending from it.

People who learn and use cognitive behavioral methods (such as those presented in this book) to decrease stress get reemployed sooner than those who don't use them (Della-Posta and Drummond 2006). Though that extra effort isn't part of the résumé, the calmness of mind and positive attitude you may gain can help you communicate with networking contacts and interviewers. Beyond the obvious benefits of projecting a positive attitude and emotions in job interviews, bringing this same positive attitude along on the job correlates with job satisfaction and tenure (Thoresen et al. 2003).

Work Experience

Write down the companies you have worked for, your title, and the key job functions you performed. You can list work experience chronologically, starting with the most recent and working backward, or group all your job functions together. You'll see how in the sample résumés that follow.

If you are a new graduate and have little work experience, note the work experience you do have, whether it's part-time or volunteer work, research you completed for courses, club membership or leadership, computer skills including any programming languages, and so on.

If you have been out of work for a while due to illness, stay-at-home parenting, job loss, and so on, provide the date range for this work in years. If you are making a career change, especially note skills that would carry over from your current field to your new field.

Educational Background

Start with your highest degree and write down the degree, name of the university, and its location along with the date you received your degree. You can omit your high-school diploma if you have a college degree.

Jot down any special training or skills you received or developed—for example, medical interviewing in Spanish, teaching nutrition and exercise to underprivileged youth, or resident advisor at your dormitory.

List any licenses or certifications you've earned. Jot down any special honors you received during your education, including your grade-point average if it was higher than 3.0 for undergraduate work; also note your class rank if you were in the top 10 percent of your graduating class.

Interests, Skills, and Accomplishments

List any special skills you have developed or accomplishments you've made. Include computer skills, civic responsibilities, and leadership positions. If you have published articles or books, or if you have won awards, write the name and date of each of these accomplishments. List any noteworthy hobbies or special interests, especially if you have special skills in these areas that can be useful on a job or can help an employer solve an ongoing problem.

Think through any experience you have with hobbies, part-time employment, volunteering, extracurricular activities, sports with your children, and so on. Jot down as much as you can remember and what skills you brought to each area.

References

Most people indicate "references are available upon request" on their résumé, so you may not need to provide specific names unless asked. If you have references from high-profile people, list them (such as a chairperson of the board at a Fortune 500 company, a Nobel Prize winner, or a famous author). If you have a contact with a high profile person or credibility with an organization, you may want to list that person/organization. Decision makers have more confidence in their hiring decisions when a well-known and credible person recommends a candidate. Remember to call or e-mail each person before listing him or her as a reference.

If you are still employed, should you plan to use your current supervisor? That's a judgment call that merits special thought. The last thing you need to happen is to have a prospective employer surprise your current employer by asking for a reference. Listing your supervisor as a reference may be a green light for human resources to go ahead and ask you what's going on. Normally, however, a prospective employer will be sensitive to this issue and only contact your supervisor after discussing the matter with you when a job offer is pending.

Asking your current supervisor to act as a reference while you are still employed has a downside, unless your employer has already talked about downsizing or mentioned that your job is due to be eliminated, which is unlikely because employers typically hold onto such information as long as they can.

If you know that your work is respected and that your current employer will have a tough time replacing you, you might be able to work out a new arrangement at a higher salary after suggesting the prospect of leaving. However, it might be best to wait to have this type of conversation until you have an offer pending.

CREATE A SMART RÉSUMÉ

Now that you have finished the brainstorming part of putting together a smart résumé, you are ready to decide which style best suits your abilities and experience. The chronological and the functional résumés are commonly used, but before we describe how to construct them, here are some general ideas and tips that came from reviewing résumés that quickly ended up in the circular file:

> Keep your résumé organized and concise. It's unrealistic to believe the reviewer is willing to wade through muddled material to figure out that you are a great candidate.

> Be sure your résumé contains correct grammar, spelling, and word usage.

> Maintain a consistent style—for example, if you start out using phrases instead of sentences, continue using phrases.

> Use standard one-inch margins. Structured use of white space adds to the attractiveness of the document.

> Quality paper sends a message. Cotton bond in white, ivory, light gray, or light blue gives a higher-quality presentation that will stand out above the everyday twenty-pound white paper that's used in printers and copiers.

> Use action verbs in active voice. Verbs like "ensured," "completed," "achieved," "engineered," "devised," and "directed" come across better than passive verb constructions, such as "was given responsibility" or "efforts were made."

> Don't assume that all organizations use the same jargon. To be on the safe side, omit jargon, abbreviations, and shop talk.

> ➤ If you mail or hand-deliver a résumé, take special care that it won't wind up folded or wrinkled upon arrival. We suggest using a nine-by-twelve-inch envelope with thin cardboard on both sides of the résumé and cover letter. It will stand out as crisper than résumés delivered folded in regular business envelopes. From a psychological perspective, this approach can convey a message that you are a conscientious candidate, and conscientiousness is normally valued.

Chronological Résumés

Earlier observations suggest that employers generally prefer chronological résumés (Morin and Yorkes 1982; Toth 1993), and even in this electronic age we observe this ongoing preference, especially for e-mail submissions. We also see a trend in which applicants use a combined chronological and functional format when the job history fits a chronological format but also includes special skills in home-office work or self-employment. Screeners are normally more comfortable reading material set in a familiar format, so this style is worth considering first.

Start with your full name, address, phone number, and e-mail address. It bears repeating to use a phone that's not shared by others, with voice mail or an answering machine so you can retrieve messages promptly.

It's usually best to use a simple-to-read, common font, such as Times Roman, Arial, or Verdana, set in a standard size, like twelve point. Fancy script fonts tend to distract.

Your name and address set you apart, so position them so that they stand out. People normally center the name and address.

Next, list your career objectives. Starting at the left margin, list your current (or most recent) position, company name, position title, and dates you worked in that position at that company. If you were promoted, list your promoted title first, then your former title along with dates within the same company listing. Continue to list each company you worked for until you reach your first full-time job. If you are fresh out of college, identify part-time or summer employment in the same manner.

Starting at the left margin, list your:

1. Work experience, dates, and titles

2. Education with degree, name of college, address of college, year graduated, and honors held, in reverse chronological order, with the most recent degree first

3. Special accomplishments and interests, community activities, professional licenses, certifications, and memberships

4. Special awards, in reverse chronological order, including date and name of award

5. References, noting any well-known people in the industry, in alphabetical order, with address and phone number; or just use the statement "Excellent references available on request".

STRUCTURING A CHRONOLOGICAL RÉSUMÉ

Samantha, a twenty-nine-year-old graphic artist, sought new employment after a plant closing. After thinking about what she really did well, she decided she liked working in the computer game industry but wanted to make sure she found a larger company with a sound financial base. Samantha decided on the objective "To create effective software product illustrations for a stable but growing computer game company." Here's her chronological résumé:

SAMANTHA BOUVIER DOE
123 Chapter Boulevard
Canton, MA 01121
555-222-1234
sdoe@youremailserver.com

CAREER OBJECTIVE:

To create effective software product illustrations for a stable but growing computer game company

WORK EXPERIENCE:

Research Assistant, New York University, New York, New York, May 2006–June 2010

- Developed illustrations for campus brochures and websites
- Assisted in development of Web materials for prospective students
- Developed graphic presentations for recruitment sessions for prospective students

EDUCATION:

- Bachelor of Fine Arts, minor in Japanese and Russian languages, New York University, New York, New York, 2009; Summa Cum Laude, Varsity Tennis, Foreign Studies, 2000, Tokyo, Japan

SPECIAL ACCOMPLISHMENTS AND INTERESTS:

- Developed illustrations for a medical interviewing guide in Japanese and Russian

COMMUNITY ACTIVITIES:

- Member, Youth Club of America
- Teaching tennis to middle-school students

PROFESSIONAL MEMBERSHIPS AND CERTIFICATIONS:

- Graphic Artists Guild

SPECIAL AWARDS:

- 2010 New York University Graphic Arts Award

INTERESTS:

- Collecting 1950s metal lunch boxes
- White-water rafting
- Coaching girls' soccer

REFERENCES: Excellent references available on request

Functional Résumés

Functional résumés are skills based, enabling you to highlight your special skills and accomplishments, and draw attention to your most marketable qualities. This résumé style works for people with a breadth of experience or multiple talents that would clutter a standard chronological résumé, gaps in employment, or special technical abilities. Professionals with gaps in their employment may prefer this style. Functional résumés may include professional experience or experience in sales, a technical field, marketing, accounting, finance, software design, or publications.

Unless carefully organized, functional résumés can disconnect skills and accomplishments from the list of employers, titles, and dates. Disconnectedness suggests a disorganized approach, which can frustrate the gatekeeper who skims your résumé.

If you carry it out thoughtfully, you can use this form of résumé to connect your job skills and employment history tastefully and show job continuity. But what happens if you have a high rate of job turnover? List the functions, followed by the names of past employers where you performed those functions. Use year-to-year dates or no dates at all.

This résumé format has a downside. Many employers are suspicious about functional résumés that mainly highlight skills but are thin on dated work history. The résumé can send up red flags if it seems that there are unexplained gaps in employment. Under these conditions, you might do better working through networking contacts who can provide credible explanations for work gaps or the appearance of a rotating-door job pattern, where you remain for a relatively short time with one employer before moving on to the next. If you can't get this assistance, a fact-based cover letter may provide explanations. Though it may suggest a spotty work history, if you have a unique and necessary skill set, the functional résumé can be a reasonable choice. A job search is partially a numbers game. The more contacts you make, the greater your chances of becoming gainfully employed.

Here's how to set up a functional résumé. After your name, address, phone number, and career objective, list your marketable skills under job categories, with your most marketable (significant) skill first; then list education, accomplishments and interests, and references. A sample functional résumé follows:

JOSEPH BLAKE
113 Merry Street
South Windsor, CT 06413
555-123-4567
Jblake@youremailservermail.com

OBJECTIVE: To contribute my knowledge in production supervision, training, and quality control to a progressive manufacturing organization

EDUCATION: Associate of Science, Green Mountain Community College
Quality Inspector Certificate, American Institute of Quality

PRODUCTION SUPERVISION EXPERIENCE: Production planning and crew supervision, quality control monitoring, development and implementation of plans to improve material flow to reduce costs and improve efficiency, maintenance, ensuring a safe work environment, establishing and maintaining positive working relationships with union members in a unionized work environment—J. F. Williams Company, Hartford, CT 07145

TRAINING AND DEVELOPMENT EXPERIENCE: Developed and implemented cross-training program for quality control and support personnel to provide opportunities for subordinates to change career paths, reducing yearly labor costs by $43,000; provided housekeeping and safety training for hourly production workers, resulting in a 35 percent reduction in lost time from accidents—Baygall Plastic Company, Windsor Locks, CT 05245

QUALITY CONTROL EXPERIENCE: Established tracking system to follow and record product quality through four control points, resulting in a 7 percent reduction in customer returns and savings of $225,896; introduced "Quality Network" program, a quality-control effort that pooled information from different groups on quality-improvement measures and improved the quality of communications among the groups—J. F. Williams Company, Hartford, CT 07145

MILITARY: U.S. Marine Corps, Honorable Discharge

REFERENCES: Excellent references available on request

USE ONLINE SOURCES EFFECTIVELY

Many organizations prefer to receive cover letters and résumés by mail, but the trend is toward electronic transmissions, such as e-mail and e-résumé transmission.

If a job advertisement asks that you respond by e-mail, it's wise to follow that procedure. If you submit your résumé in an e-mail message, someone will view your information promptly, say within twenty seconds. Include a pithy cover-letter-style statement in your e-mail, such as "I am applying for your position as district sales manager, and the following résumé shows that I amply meet your education and experience requirements."

Unless instructed otherwise, make your résumé part of the message. Some corporate e-mail filters may prevent attached résumés from being downloaded and read. However, there's a way to have the best of both worlds by typing, "My résumé follows, attached in a separate message." Then send a second message attaching your résumé for extra assurance that it will be read.

To guard against something funky happening to your résumé text formatting during transmission, we suggest running e-mail trials by sending the résumé to yourself and friends to ensure that your résumé doesn't end up at its destination looking weird. You can preserve your résumé's format by saving it as a PDF (Portable Document Format) file and attaching it to a second e-mail message.

Human resources divisions for particularly computer-literate companies, such as high-tech firms, are increasingly likely to scout for prospective employees through their preferred electronic medium. We've spoken to traditional businesses, such as paper companies, who also rely on this method of transmittal. Companies can inexpensively advertise for open positions, save money over traditional advertising, and draw job searchers from a larger geographical pool. So, look for this practice to increase.

Résumé-scanning programs allow employers to categorize résumés in their database using key words to identify candidates who list the skills needed for the position. These search engines pick up on nouns, rather than verbs, so it's important to include keywords that relate to your experience and education, optimizing your chances for review by organizations that are looking for particular keywords.

Guidelines for e-Résumés

The techniques for online posting and design of text résumés, or e-résumés, go beyond the space limitations for this book, but consider the following guidelines for expanding your search by submitting your résumé for online posting:

- ➤ Most online forms follow a chronological format, so functional résumés are typically discouraged.

- ➤ Comply with requested text formatting, which is usually an ASCII text version of your résumé because optical character recognition software can easily read such formats. But you'll have to redesign your résumé to fit this format when converting it from your word-processing program.

- ➤ Start with your name and address in capital letters centered on the page. After listing your mailing address, list your phone number on one line and then your e-mail address on a separate line.

- ➤ Use asterisks (*) or plus signs (+) instead of bullets.

- ➤ Use capital letters or boldface type instead of underlining or italics (underlining and italics don't usually scan well).

- ➤ Use the space bar instead of tabs or tables to indent. Avoid using vertical lines and boxes, and use as few horizontal lines as possible.

- ➤ Be concise. Whenever possible, limit it to one page. Otherwise, also include your name and address at the top of the second page.

- ➤ If using a résumé website that's in HTML, avoid linking your résumé to personal information, such as family pictures. Keep it pithy and professional. Consider including a keyword summary after your name and address—for example, "Keywords: engineer, management, supervision, master's degree, bachelor's degree, fluid mechanics, mechanical engineering." Keep your keyword list to fewer than fifty words.

Because rules change quickly regarding online posting, we suggest reviewing the most up-to-date guidelines for creating and formatting e-résumés—for example, type "e-résumé rules" into your favorite search engine and see what surfaces.

You can tailor either a chronological or a functional résumé to a specific job. Such modifications are typically wise, especially when you are applying directly to an employer. Using keywords that the organization features in its advertisement and applying them to your qualifications may get your résumé noticed. Few people we know use exactly the same résumé under all circumstances without adjusting it to the job. This practice is all the more important when submitting a résumé directly to a company.

Online Job-Search Opportunities

The best approach is to diversify, using all resources at your disposal, both traditional and electronic. But don't put all your eggs in one basket. A 2009 summa cum laude graduate applied to over fifty positions through online sources but received only one response, which was sent by mail and indicated that he had not been selected for the position. Is this typical?

To scientists, a single example means little, while patterns and trends are of greater value. What can be said about the value of applying for positions through online job services? An early Yankelovich poll showed that companies hired only one in ten of their new employees as a result of an online contact (Fisher 2001). However, since 2001, Internet job searches have grown to include 38 percent of unemployed and 14 percent of employed job searchers (Brown 2008), so we think there's some potential in posting your credentials on a job-search website. But don't rely exclusively on this method.

Differing statistics and studies identifying the effectiveness of looking for a job online show inconsistent results. Although you can find increasing numbers of job-search websites, the data regarding how many people searching online actually find a job that way is fuzzy. For example, some job searchers say that using an online résumé database is like placing your résumé in a "black hole," never to be heard from again. Others find work this way. There seems to be little downside to posting your résumé online, but once you post it, it's on public view, so post only what you don't mind having others see.

LETTERS THAT SELL

Having finished your résumé and found a job posting that sounds good, chances are you will have to correspond with prospective employers. Writing a quality cover letter adds support to your résumé.

The purpose of written correspondence is to express your interest and availability and to highlight your unique qualifications and link them to the position. You also will need to create letters for other purposes, including responding to advertised jobs, introducing yourself to search firms, formally requesting assistance from contacts who can advise you or refer you to a decision maker, and thanking those who helped you or interviewed you.

Framing Your Letter

Letters to prospective employers are normally one page long and contain a sequence of elements: (1) your reason for writing, (2) why the reader should feel interested in meeting with you, (3) the type of position you want and what you have accomplished to merit the role, (4) your interest in working with this organization, (5) a statement of intent, and (6) the attachments you enclosed.

Unless you seek the position of corporate officer, you might get more attention by directing your letter, by name, to the vice president in charge of your specialty. Mark the letter "personal and confidential." The following sample letter follows this format:

JANE W. DOE
15 Cobble Drive
Dixon, MT 02121
701-123-1234
Jdoe7Q1@youremailserver.com

May 20, 2010

Mark R. Smith, Vice President of Marketing
Lady's Wear Incorporated
23 Warren Avenue
Billingswood, CO 80721

Dear Mr. Smith:

I want to apply for the position of advertising manager listed in this morning's *Wall Street Journal*. I first contacted Mr. Larry Smith, who directed me to your office.

Through recent news articles, I learned that your company's newly patented Busy Lady stretch-hose product line will revolutionize the hosiery market because of your patented "no-tear" feature. Busy Lady is a unique product with exceptional potential to gain market dominance.

I have fourteen years of documented success in marketing and advertising hosiery products. I know the market and what to do to connect consumers with sellers. I want to put this knowledge to work to make Busy Lady the best-selling hosiery brand. If I were your advertising manager, you could feel confident that I would carefully target your advertising to reach potential consumers and generate more sales.

I plan to phone your office next week to see if I might speak with you about this exciting opportunity. Thank you for your consideration. My résumé is attached.

Very truly yours,

Jane W. Doe

Rules of Thumb for Cover Letters

Use the same type of paper and font for the letter as you did for the résumé, and continue using active verbs and conciseness. Avoid jargon and slang.

Be consistent, and get the letter and résumé out to the gatekeeper as soon as possible after you see the advertisement. If the employer doesn't express a preference for conventional mail over electronic transmission and you are nearby, consider hand-delivering the letter and résumé. This shows initiative, and besides, you may pick up some additional information about the organization. If you have to mail your materials, consider using USPS Priority Mail. Call within a few days to follow up on receipt of your letter. Another option is to fax your cover letter and résumé with a note that original copies will follow by mail.

When you use a template for a letter in which you include company names in the text, triple-check to ensure that you don't have the name of the wrong company embedded in the text.

STRATEGIES FOR SUCCESS

Now that you've jotted down some notes, which style of résumé do you think works best for you? Can you use one or more of the samples and strategies to develop a first draft?

KEY IDEAS

1.

2.

3.

ACTION STEPS

1.

2.

3.

IMPLEMENTATION

1.

2.

3.

RESULTS

1.

2.

3.

POSTSCRIPT

A smart résumé is a step toward your goal of finding the great job you deserve—one that fits your skills, abilities, and interests. What's more, it helps you gather momentum in your job search. You now have a vehicle to move you to the next step, a job interview. In chapters 7 and 8 you'll see how to continue on your success track by using psychological strategies to communicate with positive impact in interviews.

7 GET TO THE DECISION MAKERS

Reaching and getting interviews with gatekeepers and decision makers is the payoff for all the hard work you've done up to this point. Who are the gatekeepers? Members of this group include anyone who can get you in the door to give you the chance to make your case. Networking through your personal and business contacts is a highly productive way to locate job opportunities for blue-collar, white-collar, management, and professional positions (Wanberg, Kanfer, and Banas 2000).

You have many ways to get through to gatekeepers; as the proverb goes, "leave no stone unturned." Anyone you know who may know someone who can get you in front of a decision maker is a gatekeeper. A friend who knows of a potential opening and whom you can contact at the organization is a potential gatekeeper, as may also be an acquaintance you meet at a party or members of your job-search club.

Networking is a major way to get through the gate and have your credentials taken seriously by decision makers. We've found that hiring authorities tend to prefer to hire candidates recommended by people they know and in whom they have confidence.

We recognize that fearless job hunters have a broad range of social styles and temperaments. Some will find networking more compatible with their style than others will. Nevertheless, networking tends to be productive. We encourage you to experiment with this approach even if, at first, networking feels uncomfortable. With practice, this method will likely lead to your developing your skills and becoming more comfortable with networking. We'll share with you how to build productive networking and other contact systems and how to maintain relationships with these important resources.

There are many ways to get the same result, and some ways are more comfortable to carry out than others. Responding to a job advertisement with a résumé is probably more comfortable than networking, cold-calling, working with search firms, creating consulting opportunities, and using e-mail to support a job search. But if your goal is to intensely and persistently turn over as many promising stones as possible, applying multiple strategies to achieve the single result of getting a great job will likely produce multiple opportunities. Nevertheless, emphasizing more productive networking approaches over wait-and-see newspaper advertisement opportunities puts you in a stronger position to control your job-search process.

NETWORK FOR SUCCESS

Decision makers or gatekeepers are the people who decide who gets to be interviewed and who doesn't. It's crucial to develop strategies that will maximize your efforts to not only impress the decision maker but also get you to the interviewing process.

Most of the jobs people get are derived from business and personal contacts. Being able to network effectively and take advantage of these sources is critical. Networking is also advantageous to the companies looking to hire for a key position, because they can save on advertising and search-firm fees.

Networking is, time and again, a solid route to follow, and projecting a positive attitude can make a favorable difference. Marjorie tells us:

> I had absolutely nothing to lose, because the beauty of not having a job is that you can try anything. Everywhere I went, I let people know I was looking, and I asked for names of others who could possibly help me. I met some fabulous people along the way, and we formed a support group whose purpose was to find jobs for all the members. As a group we collectively looked for ways to get out and get interviews. I got a great job, and so did most of the group.

When you have nothing to lose, it's surprising what you can accomplish. So when you lose your job, celebrate, because it's an opportunity to experiment to see what works, and you can share what you learned and did with others who seek a great job.

QUICK TIPS

➤ Keep your networking focused on getting to decision makers.

➤ Be mindful of the type of work atmosphere where you are likely to thrive, and give weight to organizations that best exemplify those conditions.

➤ Identify skills that are helpful in getting to a decision maker, and start strengthening these skills.

➤ Prompt yourself to view as a challenge each phase of the process of finding the gatekeeper.

➤ Use feelings of discomfort about following through with key parts of your search as catalysts for action.

➤ Boost your self-awareness skills through reflectively identifying and correcting consistent errors, such as speaking too quickly.

➤ Use *Fearless Job Hunting* and other sources of information to get and keep a winning edge.

The minute you start talking to friends, relatives, and business contacts, you are networking to get to the appropriate gatekeeper. The key to success in this area is to connect with as many people as possible. One or more will help open the door for a critical interview, and some may make inquiries for you among gatekeepers they know.

You can divide your networking contacts into primary and secondary groups. The primary sources are the people who have a higher likelihood of connecting you with someone who knows where you can find a job or knows whom you might call for help. These are the people who know you and can refer you with confidence. Most jobs are filled as a result of direct contacts. Secondary sources may have some potential to get you a job, but on a fearless search, your full-time job is to find a job. The bottom line is this: put most of your time into networking to create good contacts.

Use Your Primary Sources Effectively

Here are some tips for identifying and soliciting the help of primary resources:

> Contact recently promoted executives. Promotions are often announced in newspapers. These individuals may want to put their mark on their department by making some personnel changes and bringing new people on board.

> Contact recently hired or promoted individuals for their leads. Now that they are in their new jobs, they still possess valuable contact names that they no longer need. Some of these people would pass along their leads to you if you asked them.

> Send a cover letter and several copies of your résumé to the alumni placement director of the college or university you attended. Companies often contact directors in search of names of people with specific skills.

> If an organization is not advertising for a position, don't assume the door is closed. Approach directors of personnel, human resources managers, and employee relations directors to ask about expected job openings. They have all the information inside their organization about potential job openings that arise due to retirements, promotions, and other job changes. Your proactive approach may impress them to the point where they offer you a job interview to save the time and money they would have spent to advertise an upcoming position. Also you may ask them for search methods they have used and could recommend. They often have a list of resources they regularly use.

> Speak to any contacts or resources you encounter, such as your insurance agent, your hairstylist or barber, your accountant,

your banker, your former teachers, your professors, community leaders, local political representatives, your family physician, your dentist, relatives, acquaintances, your next-door neighbor, former employees, your financial planner, any salespeople you encounter when you go shopping, and cab drivers. In other words, anyone you meet whom you know and who knows you is a potential source for leads.

➤ Especially contact friends, relatives, and acquaintances who have recently changed jobs. They can offer insights into what actions worked for them and also pass along leads to you that haven't yet been approached.

Use Your Secondary Resources Effectively

In keeping with the "leave no stone unturned" theme, look wherever you have even a remote possibility of making a meaningful contact that can point you in a productive direction. Here are some ways to find secondary resource opportunities:

➤ Search through all the names in your business-card file, address file, and appointment books for potential leads and opportunities.

➤ Regularly attend seminars, lectures, trade association meetings, and conferences where you can meet people, some of whom may turn into valuable contacts. Exchange business cards and follow up with these contacts by sending a cover letter along with your résumé.

➤ Contact others you know who are also searching for new employment. They may know of leads in your field that can benefit you.

➤ You may also consider establishing a small support group of people who are looking for jobs (a job-search club), to exchange leads and search techniques that work and to invite guest speakers who have found interesting jobs to talk about the innovative techniques they employed to secure their positions.

➤ Make contact with acquaintances, friends, and colleagues who have found a new job to uncover opportunities at their previous companies.

➤ Regularly scan the business section of the newspaper. Send a congratulatory letter to recently hired or newly promoted decision makers; include your résumé, and follow up with a phone call.

➤ Use the Internet or your community library to identify public and nonprofit organizations where you would like to work. Examine their annual reports to gain more knowledge about the organization. Then decide which decision maker you plan to approach. Construct a letter introducing yourself, declaring your strong desire to work there, and describing the contribution you could make to the organization. Follow up with a phone call.

➤ Use the U.S. Department of Labor website at www.dol.gov for information on available positions and how to complete an application for a federal job.

➤ Contact retired executives or managers and request their advice and assistance with your search for decision makers.

➤ Consider part-time or contract work for a company to get your foot in the door and impress the decision maker enough to offer you a full-time position.

➤ Take a job at a telemarketing company during the interim between your career jobs. It will provide you with a small income and, more importantly, will allow you to practice your telephone skills.

Work Effectively with Your Contacts

The process of finding and working with contacts is an important exercise that warrants special attention. Like most interpersonal situations, a diplomatic but persistent approach typically yields better results.

Check out Ben Franklin's autobiography. His eighteenth-century wisdom about using the language of diplomacy is still valid. In a nutshell, he advised using wording that avoids putting you or others on the spot (Franklin 1986).

Steve recalls his search for decision makers:

I became a pain in the butt, and that hurt me. I lost a few friends along the way. This process of hunting down leads consumed me. That's all I ever thought about and talked about. I wouldn't leave it alone. My wife even got fed up and was afraid to have people over at the house. I eventually got a job and celebrated the occasion with some friends and relatives. One of my closest friends pulled me aside and told me how happy he was that I got a job because he couldn't stand being around me any longer. I learned a lesson, and that's to pace yourself, and although people want to help, your problem is not theirs and you should respect their limitations.

Here are some tips for communicating with the people who can help you the most:

➤ Choose people who are familiar with your industry and the key players in it.

➤ Make certain your contacts know your capabilities and skills and what position you seek, so that when they have an opportunity to describe your qualifications, they can do so confidently and accurately.

➤ Be sure to choose contacts who are willing to help you when you simply ask them to, without your having to twist an arm. What may surprise you is that at times, acquaintances can be more helpful than relatives.

➤ Set yourself a reasonable target, such as getting two leads from each person you meet.

➤ When you approach people, you can tend to get too caught up in your search for decision makers and may inadvertently take up too much of your contact's time. Be sensitive to people's time, limitations, and willingness to cooperate.

➤ Treat every contact courteously and professionally.

➤ Once you receive help, communicate your gratitude with a thank-you note. If someone has gone above and beyond the call of duty, it's normally suitable to offer a small gift that fits that person's interests.

➤ After you have found a job, inform your contacts. They will appreciate hearing your success story.

➤ Remember, when approached, most people will help to some degree if they can. However, some may not be able or want to help at all and would feel bothered if you even asked them for the time of day. But when there's an opportunity to develop a quality contact, try it, without acting pushy.

If a contact decides to help, this is a discretionary act. Acknowledging the use of his or her time and your appreciation for that effort is normally wiser than acting like a fawning sycophant. Confident contacts will more likely lend assistance to people who are capable of helping themselves and who follow up quickly on their leads.

RESEARCH EMPLOYERS

Research is most important because it's how you find the decision makers to pursue. When you arm yourself with information about an organization, you present as a more credible candidate.

In this information age, you can tap multiple resources to advance your search for decision makers with influence or hiring authority. Your local library has reference volumes that describe companies and their boards, trade associations, and officers. Then there are public, university, and college libraries; board of trade libraries; and computer databases that allow you to search for information about companies and their key executives. Here's a sampling of resources to access from your local library or, in some cases, the Internet. (Note: Public libraries provide free resources, and some have extensive career libraries and references. Accessing similar documents from the Internet, such as *Value Line* and *Thomas Register,* can be pricey. If this cost comes at a time when you are out of work and short on funds, the public resources are good for the price.)

➤ *Standard and Poor's Register of Corporations, Directors, and Executives* lists tens of thousands of corporations and their board members, executives, directors, and other senior members. The information about the executives and directors includes title, education, business address, and other valuable data, making it possible for you to contact them in a meaningful way. This publication may be available at your local library. As an alternative, consider a free trial at hoovers.com, which has a database with comparable information.

➤ *Thomas Register of American Manufacturers* offers company profiles, products, and services. By accessing this data, you can carefully target the corporations that have jobs aligned with your interests and skill set. Prior printed versions are available in most community libraries at no cost. When you suspect some information may be dated, you can normally get onto company websites to identify key or recent changes. We advise double-checking the company website to ensure that your contacts are up-to-date.

➤ *The Value Line Investment Survey* reports on and rates about seventeen hundred corporations. It lists the various types of businesses by industry and determines their stability. This information will allow you to pursue decision makers who work in reliable and growing organizations. If an organization looks as if it's on a slippery slope toward bankruptcy, this information can be critical. Because online subscription fees can be costly for a job seeker with limited finances, you can view an up-to-date *Value Line* document at most local libraries.

➤ *Encyclopedia of Associations* provides valuable information about professional organizations and trade associations. Associations often act as intermediaries between job hunters and company decision makers and don't charge either party. It's a service they provide to their association membership. If you aren't a member of a professional association, it might be in your best interest to join one. You'll find associations listed that match your professional pursuits. If you are a member, regularly check your newsletter or journal for career opportunities, and also contact your association representatives for up-to-date prospects.

➤ Corporate annual reports are informative. They offer a complete picture of the organization, including its key board members, executives, current status, growth opportunities, challenges, future directions, and financial health. When you approach decision makers and show that you have a good knowledge of this background information, they'll see that you've done your homework.

➤ If you have a stock brokerage account that gives you access to company reports, you can benefit from information about an organization's financial strength, products, competitors, growth, and so on.

➤ Company newsletters are often offered by larger and some medium-sized companies. They highlight events, accomplishments, employee moves, and significant success stories, giving you a snapshot of the organization's culture. This data can help you refine your résumé, tailor your cover letter, and prepare for a potential interview. You might be able to obtain copies by requesting recent issues from the organization's human resources department.

➤ Magazines such as *Forbes, Fortune, BusinessWeek*, and *Inc.* and newspapers such as the *Wall Street Journal* and *Barron's* offer ideas about companies to research and people to contact. Some list prominent companies, successful companies, and growing organizations. *Inc.*, for example, catalogues the 100 fastest-growing companies—and with growth comes more hiring.

Though you may start your search with limited knowledge about how to research organizations for employment opportunities, as you gather information through the Internet, the library, newspaper archives, and other sources, you'll likely gain insight about how to identify and analyze organizations that merit your attention.

The time you spend researching organizations can pay dividends. The library is a great resource for gathering information. Gatekeepers and decision makers are more likely to be impressed by knowledgeable applicants than by people who want a job but haven't taken the time to study the organization or determine much about the company and its people, products, initiatives, and competitors.

Organize Your Research Material

During your quest for the key decision makers, it's necessary to organize your information so that it's easily accessible, up-to-date, and categorized by company. Because you will track a number of companies at the same time, this is all the more reason to systematize rather than rely on your memory. If you prefer not to handwrite the information, use a word-processing program to maintain the record.

SEARCH FIRMS AND WHAT THEY SEARCH FOR

Recruitment firms typically range in size from one- to two-person operations to large international organizations with hundreds of employees. Some are listed on the various stock exchanges.

Recruitment firms can be either retainer or contingency firms. The retainer firms get money up front from organizations seeking a special candidate, whereas the contingency firms make money if they place you.

Contingency Firms

Contingency firms are recruiters who receive payment from the employer contingent upon successfully placing a candidate in their organization. As such, they will employ a shotgun approach. If you are their client, they will send you to as many companies as possible for interviews, hoping that one organization will indeed hire you. They also use this approach to impress upon their employers that they can produce many suitable candidates.

There's a secondary benefit: by attending a number of interviews, you practice your interview skills. But to save you some time and effort, it may be in your best interest to examine with the recruiter the company's requirements and whether there's a good fit between what you offer and the company's specifications before you go on the interview. You'll save yourself and the organization time and trouble if it's clear that the fit isn't there.

Retainer Firms

Retainer firms begin the recruiting process once they are given a job assignment, and they usually receive a large payment or retainer from the employer for their services. If the services are extremely complex, the search fee can get quite expensive. Retainer firms conduct their own research, do background checks, and seek recommendations before approaching a candidate for the position. The candidate is usually an employed, highly educated top performer of some prominence, with an open ear to better career possibilities. Retainer firm specialists try to induce a candidate to leave one firm and join their client's firm. Larger retainer firms have offices located in major cities around the world.

These firms are only interested in candidates who closely fit the requirements of the position and are in a certain income bracket. They usually contract for searches where the employee requires a minimum annual salary from sixty to seventy-five thousand dollars and higher.

Unless you have top-notch credentials and a very strong reason for being unemployed, such as a corporate restructuring or takeover, it may be difficult to gain entry into one of these larger search firms. But that shouldn't stop you from approaching them. Like most parts of a job search, this is a numbers game. The more doors you knock on, the more likely one will open. If you have a strong reputation as a go-getter, and you have in-demand skills, the recruiter may arrange to meet with you.

Research the Search Firm

Search or recruitment firms are there to find you a job. They attempt to match the candidate to the most suitable positions. There are numerous firms available, some with better reputations than others, some with longer track records than others, and, finally, some with higher ethical standards than others. They are listed in the yellow pages of the phone book, many have websites, and a few strongly advertise their services in the want ads of your local newspaper. Some recruiters have a national presence, with offices around the country, while others, considered boutique firms, are more local and often specialize in the professionals they place.

When locating a search firm, do your research first. Ask people who have had experience with recruiters for their impressions. Visit websites and approach firms that have been in business for a considerable period of time. Try to locate those firms that place people with your specialty. Visit a few firms and determine your comfort level. Finally, avoid firms that expect you to pay a fee for placement, and use only those that get paid by the employer. Some unethical enterprises charge you a stiff fee and then also charge the organization if they place you.

Following are some resources to help you locate a good search firm:

➤ Check out your community library for a directory of recruitment firms.

➤ If you are an executive, you may find useful information at the Association of Executive Search Consultants website: www.aesc .org. Review the latest edition of *The Directory of Executive and Professional Recruiters* (published by Kennedy Information).

➤ Contact the human resources departments of companies you have targeted. Inform them that you are interested in working for their organization, but given that there are no opportunities currently available, you would like the name of the search firm they use, the name of a contact within the firm, and their impressions about the firm. This conversation has two benefits: you get the name of a search firm and, equally important, if not more so, you establish a presence. Should the company have a future opening, human resources may call you directly to avoid the recruitment fee.

Build a Relationship with the Key Contact at Your Search Firm

You are worth money to the search firm if, and only if, the firm can place you. It's your job, then, to sell the search firm on what you bring to the table so that it can, in turn, sell you to respective companies.

Make it worth the search firm's time and effort to promote you by promoting yourself and giving them the confidence that they can successfully represent you. Your skills, your competencies, and your experience are the elements that will allow them to make money by finding you a worthwhile job. So be sure to do a lot for them to make their job easier. You'll also want to get clear on what they plan to do for you so you can reach your employment objectives.

Before you contact the search firm, prepare a brief pitch about who you are and what you can offer, and incorporate this into the conversation to capture the recruiter's attention.

The recruiter will likely ask you a variety of questions, so make certain to prepare yourself so you won't be caught off guard. The recruiter may ask you questions like the following:

- What is your background?

- What are your interests?

- What's your availability?

- What salary are you looking for?

- What are your strengths?

- What areas do you need to develop?

- How are you different from other candidates?

- What do you bring to a company?

- How do you plan to overcome your limitations (such as limited education or lack of experience)?

The recruiter will sometimes ask awkward questions to see how well you handle them and how composed you are in the process. Recruiters also ask these questions and others as a way to prep you for upcoming interviews.

You may choose to use more than one recruiter, which has advantages and disadvantages. More than one firm may try to place you in the same position to get the placement fee, which can be awkward. Once a search firm discovers that you are working with a number of firms and haven't declared it, this may cause animosity and present serious problems to you if you ever want to use any of the involved firms in the future.

A second issue that can surface is when your recruiter presents you to a company where there's a good fit, but the company suddenly declines the application and decides to advertise privately because the search fee is too high. You then respond to the advertisement, and, because there's no search fee attached, the company now favorably responds to your application. The search firm may still be entitled to a fee.

By declaring any potential conflict of interest at the outset of the agreement between you and the recruiter, you each know where the other stands, mitigating the possibility of complications down the road.

THE DIRECT-MAIL CAMPAIGN

A direct-mail campaign involves sending out letters to numerous companies to increase the possibility of getting a job interview. Jill summed up her mailing campaign this way:

> *I made a point of compiling the names of senior contacts in five hundred companies. I researched each company very carefully at the board of trade library, choosing only companies that I've always wanted to work for or that interested me. It took a while, but it was worth it. I put together a solid but brief letter pointing out my desire to work at each company—which was true; otherwise I wouldn't have chosen the organization. I sent out twenty-five letters a week and followed each letter with a phone call. I got five interviews and two job offers. Now, it seems like a lot of work, but it was really worth it, because I got a fabulous job and learned a lot about myself—namely, if I want something badly enough, I'm very capable of working hard to get it!*

Here are six steps to a successful direct-mail campaign:

1. Research and record information on companies you wish to pursue. These will likely be organizations that truly appeal to you, including many that fit your skill set, plus some that may not fit your skill set but are of strong interest to you.

2. Develop your mailing list by using the research resources at your community library or college or university library.

3. Be certain to identify the key person in the organization to whom you plan to address your letter. A "to whom it may concern" letter will most likely go straight into the "circular file."

4. Prepare a letter of interest, indicating your strong desire to work for that particular company and inquiring about the possibility of getting an interview to explore current and future employment prospects. Use the style presented in chapter 6 for your letter of introduction.

5. Be sure to customize your letters so they don't give the appearance of a bulk mailing. Also, if you use a template, double-check your content to avoid using more than one company name in the text.

6. Follow up your letter with a phone call three to five days later. Skipping this step will water down the benefits of your mailing campaign. Although it may take significant time and effort to reach the key person, working your way through receptionists, administrative assistants, and even human resources personnel may help you establish potential networking contacts.

THE COLD-CALLING CAMPAIGN

Cold-calling involves making an unsolicited call to a person inside an organization whom you don't know and have never spoken to before. Because it typically has a low yield regarding getting a job, cold-calling is seldom used. In keeping with our "leave no stone unturned" theme, consider that mining this area might produce a favorable result. This approach may not fit your temperament, but practice makes a positive difference. Once you climb far enough up the cold-calling learning curve, your sophistication in this approach increases your chances of getting a job interview and offer.

We suggest starting with low-interest organizations that look for applicants with similar talents to yours. When the time comes to contact organizations you are more interested in, you'll be better prepared. You also get the side benefit of preparing yourself to feel comfortable and competent when it comes time to interview.

Because many people find cold-calling very uncomfortable, they avoid it. Once you start making cold calls, you'll clearly have a leg up over competitors who shy away from this approach. Frank was bold in his approach to cold calls:

> *I put a pitch together that basically said who I was, that I wanted to work for this particular company for the following reasons, and that I wanted to have a meeting to see how we could make it happen. From the fifteen calls I made, I got six interviews and three job offers. I guess I blew them away with my approach. I had nothing to lose!*

Here are four steps to making successful cold calls:

1. Research the companies you wish to pursue. This will also help you be quicker on your feet when responding to questions.

2. Identify the key people to speak to in the various organizations. If you can't identify a gatekeeper, ask the company operator who's available to speak to you.

3. Prepare a short script and rehearse it a number of times to get comfortable. Then put the script aside when you call, to avoid sounding too rehearsed. The script should contain who you are, why you're calling, how what the company stands for and your values and competencies fit together, and a request for an interview to discuss current or future job possibilities.

4. Remind yourself that the more calls you make, the easier it becomes. This doesn't mean that you won't encounter some nasty responses, but you may also be pleasantly surprised by unusual cordiality. The more cordial organizations may be worth the extra effort to pursue.

STRATEGIES FOR SUCCESS

Getting to decision makers is a most important activity, so it's crucial to stay focused, motivated, and active in planning your next steps to eventually reach your ultimate goal of getting a great job.

KEY IDEAS

1.

2.

3.

ACTION STEPS

1.

2.

3.

IMPLEMENTATION

1.

2.

3.

RESULTS

1.

2.

3.

POSTSCRIPT

Devising an organized approach for getting to the gatekeepers and decision makers favorably distinguishes you from other job hunters, because it offers a greater and more powerful measure of regulating what you do and how you do it, ultimately helping you achieve your goal of getting to the right people.

PART 3

Close the Deal by Contacting Decision Makers, Presenting Effectively, and Negotiating Your Contract

8 SHAPE UP YOUR COMMUNICATION SKILLS

Tom holds a middle-management position and believes he's ready for an executive role. With no room to move or grow in his current job, he looks outside of his organization for his next great job.

Tom's résumé is good enough to attract positive attention—he has great references and cites exceptional accomplishments. However, over a three-year period, he garners eighty-eight job interviews and no offers. What's going on? He lacks a positive presence during his interviews.

Tom presents himself as if he deserves the job and as if company officials should get down on their knees and beg him to work for them. Thus, he blunders in interviews by projecting a defensive and arrogant demeanor.

Although many candidates undersell themselves, Tom approaches each interview as if it's an opportunity to extol his considerable virtues. His consistent error is believing he has to act dominant and in control to get a higher-level position. Fortunately, this is correctable, but to make the correction, he must realign how he thinks and operates during an interview to a brand-new perception of reality.

QUICK TIPS

➤ Establish rapport by listening attentively and responding effectively.

➤ Focus on what you want to accomplish, which is to get the job.

➤ Maintain a comfortable social distance.

➤ Maintain eye contact without staring.

➤ Watch for changes in the interviewer's tone and body language, and adapt.

➤ Avoid interrupting the interviewer in the middle of a sentence.

➤ Present in a personable and knowledgeable manner.

➤ Ask questions to surface organizational problems that you can help correct.

➤ Paraphrase to assure that you understand the interviewer's message.

If you saw Tom at work, you'd see a person who listens well and responds to subordinates' suggestions. He shows a diplomatic sharpness and ably demonstrates that he can sell his well-thought-out ideas to his supervisors. When he takes charge of projects, he shows executive-level ability. So, in a familiar setting, Tom feels relaxed and operates at his best.

Tom's solution for getting past his consistent-error hurdle is surprisingly simple. Once he becomes aware of the error, he makes a radical shift in the way he approaches the interview. He picks up a few tips that we'll describe in this chapter.

By the time Tom finishes interview number ninety-one, he has skillfully applied reflective communication skills and interacted effectively with interviewers. At interview number 102, he receives a great job offer and takes it. He attributes this turnaround result to building his reflective communication skills.

Tom has a natural sense of command and superior ability to organize and coordinate business operations. By intentionally adding new dimensions to his already fine communication skills, Tom gets great cooperation from his peers, superiors, and subordinates. He eventually becomes the chief executive officer for the organization, and the stockholders are the next group that's happy with the results.

PERSUASIVE AND REFLECTIVE COMMUNICATION

We can divide communication into two major types, each with a distinct purpose and predominant strategy. Both are useful and appropriate in certain situations, though reflective communication generally works best in interpersonal situations, such as job interviews.

The purpose of *persuasive communication* is to convince the other person to agree with your point. This is an assertiveness approach for winning an argument. Following this approach, you convince or sell. If the other person doesn't buy what you're selling, you conclude that you haven't expressed yourself well enough or the other person missed the point, so you keep hammering away.

A big part of a job interview is to share information about yourself and convince the decision maker that you are the best candidate for the job. But in persuasive communication, there's little reflective observation, going with the flow, or developing a partnership with the other person. The danger of a win-at-any-cost strategy is that you'll come across as aggressive, insensitive, and arrogant. That was Tom's consistent error. Although this approach may get you points if you are applying for a boiler-room position to sell insurance or stocks over the phone, these impressions are normally the exact opposite of the impression you want to convey.

Appearance does matter and is an important part of ensuring that you make a good impression. But appearance is more than how you dress. Tom's appearance was top notch; he dressed for success. His attitude, however, created the wrong impression and, thus, needed a radical adjustment involving reflective communication.

Radically different from persuasive communication, *reflective communication* is based on the work of psychologist Carl Rogers, particularly his client-centered therapy system (Rogers 1961). This communication style includes creating conditions to better understand the situation; to position yourself to make mindful, cogent responses; to help yourself meet your goals; and to allow the other person to feel affirmed. Such conditions are reflective and engaging, concern sharing information, and also include the often-neglected emotional areas of communication.

In reflective communication you may paraphrase for clarification and understanding—for example, "If I heard you correctly, you are looking for someone who can come into the organization and troubleshoot problems concerning your key accounts." In general, people like to believe they have been understood, and selective paraphrasing to be sure you've understood the other person serves that purpose.

Observation: Watching the Interviewer

Most people are poor at observing what's before their eyes—often because they are absorbed in something else, such as trying too hard to show their assets or worrying too much about how well they are projecting. The parable of the monk suggests how we can miss the obvious:

After three years of study, the novice monk arrives at his teacher's dwelling. He enters the room, bursting with ideas about knotty issues of Buddhist metaphysics and well prepared for the deep questions that await him in his examination.

"I have but one question," his teacher says.

"I am ready, Master," the monk replies.

"In the doorway, were the flowers to the left or to the right of the umbrella?"

The novice realizes he must go back for three more years of study.

You limit your awareness when you think too much about yourself and lose sight of what's going on around you. At times, the most important information is right before your eyes in the form of the interviewer's body language or in the way the interviewer has chosen to decorate the office. For now, here are some body-language tips to help you improve these useful observational skills:

> *Alert yourself to nonverbal cues.* According to body-language expert Ray Birdwhistell (1970), we convey 65 percent of our messages through nonverbal expression. An interviewer who leans toward you is likely showing interest. But finger tapping can convey impatience. Reflective communicators are aware of the body-language cues they send, and they work to keep a positive posture.

> *The person's posture tells part of the story.* Does the interviewer's posture change over time? Are the interviewer's pupils open wider than you'd expect for the lighting? Pupils dilate with interest and contract with anger.

> *Changes in an interviewer's posture can have a special meaning.* If you see the interviewer stiffen up from a relaxed posture, this shows an emotional response. However, the interviewer may have stiffened at the thought of something that has nothing to do with you. This might be an unconscious habit.

> *Hand gestures normally flow with the person's ideas and fit those thoughts.* Positive hand gestures include open hands and forward posture. However, the interviewer may not use his or her hands or change posture during the interview. Reflective communicators are aware of their own hand gestures. If your hand gestures appear out of rhythm with your speech, that can be distracting. Natural gestures convey a positive message.

> When a person swallows or gulps, yawns, looks away, or tightens the facial muscles, this may convey a message of tension or disinterest. If you notice any of these negative signs, it's wise to again focus on reflective communication. Ideally, you want the interviewer to feel comfortable with you. If you zone out on nonverbal cues, you lose important information that will help you present yourself positively during the interview.

While actively observing the interviewer's nonverbal style, here are two pitfalls worth noting:

> *Taking the interviewer's nonverbal style personally.* If you read too much into a situation, you may operate more on assumption and miss the picture. But accepting what you see while avoiding taking the interviewer's body language too personally lets you use your powers of observation to greater advantage. Life's too short to get mired in possibilities when concrete opportunities lie before you.

> *Occupying yourself with minutia.* Concentrating your attention on each subtle movement of the interviewer, and trying to figure out what it means, can come across as intrusive.

You will likely pick up on tone and body language if you are mindful of them, but evaluating them is an inexact science.

Be Aware of Tone

We use many sensory channels to deliver information to the mind's eye. Reflective communication involves paying close attention not only to what an interviewer says but also to how it's said. Word choice, tone, and inflection are part of the message.

Your observations of what an interviewer says and how it's said can give you an edge. If you see that the interview is going well, you can confidently continue. If you perceive a negative shift in the interviewer's tone, there's still time to promote a positive change.

Your observations can go beyond the visible when you note what tone or content is absent from a dialogue that would normally be present. Tone awareness can help you take advantage of this information to advance your chance of getting a job offer without distracting you or the interviewer. How does the interviewer sound? How can you take advantage of this observation?

Observe Yourself

While you are casually but unobtrusively observing the significance of what's happening around you, consider your own body language:

> *Are you developing eye contact early?* Look into the person's eyes, not just at his or her face. Avoid staring or looking out of the corners of your eyes. The former may cause you to appear intrusive, while the latter may cause the interviewer to believe you aren't trustworthy.

> *Are you keeping a comfortable distance?* In U.S. culture, three feet is a comfortable distance for informal discussions. But, take your cue from the interviewer.

> *Are you leaning toward the interviewer?* Leaning slowly toward the interviewer sends a positive signal, while leaning away sends a negative one.

> *Are you showing open posturing?* If you appear open and confident, that message will radiate; sit upright or slightly toward the interviewer, with your hands at your sides or sitting loosely on your lap. If you fold your arms over your chest, you may appear defiant or challenging.

Listen Attentively

Communication experts tell us that most of us are, at best, poor listeners. If we listen at all, we tend to listen either selectively (hearing only the parts that interest us) or with the intent to reply (preparing what we want to say in return). Either way, our focus is still on us. The result is that we often don't really hear valuable information. Moreover, we can easily make the other person feel as if we have no interest in what he or she is saying.

In reflective listening, you shift the focus from yourself and put your energy into the message sent by the other person. The intent is to understand the ideas the person is trying to convey and the feelings she or he may be experiencing. Key reflective listening strategies include observing, listening attentively, seeking clarification, and expressing yourself effectively.

Listening attentively is hard work. Why? You have a natural tendency to listen to another through the prism of your own experiences.

Developing an observant way of seeing and listening is a different process. Stephen Covey (1989) suggests four communication styles to avoid:

> ➢ Evaluating by agreeing or disagreeing

> ➢ Probing by asking questions from your point of view

> ➢ Advising by making suggestions from your prior experiences

> ➢ Interpreting by making assumptions about others' motivation

Here are tips for avoiding those pitfalls and sharpening your attentive-listening skills:

> ➢ When you are interviewing for a position, follow the interviewer's lead. If the interviewer begins with small talk, pick up on the person's interests.

> ➢ Watch your audience. Continue your comments when you see positive responses, but don't continue if the interviewer shows signs of tension or inattention. Saying too much can harm your case as much as saying too little.

> ➢ When an interviewer seems interested in a point you made, stop and ask if you can fill in further details.

> ➢ Periodically check back with the interviewer about what he or she is asking, whether you fully responded, and so on: "Is there anything else you'd like to know about how I might contribute to Mount Saint Helens Mining Company?"

> ➢ Focus on what the speaker says. Resist inserting your thoughts on the subject until you understand the issue. (Most of us violate this step.)

> ➢ Avoid presenting information prematurely. Answer questions fully, but don't add additional information unless the interviewer asks. For example, when describing one of your strengths, mentioning one additional strength may be okay, but stringing together examples could be considered long-winded.

Get Clarification

Even when you are reasonably confident that you have accurately tuned in to an interviewer's message, you might want to confirm what you think, to be sure your assumptions are accurate. Reflective communicators take the time to ensure they understand what the interviewer is getting at.

First, paraphrase the ideas the interviewer expresses. Start this clarification process by saying, "I hear you saying…," "It sounds as if you are saying…," or "Is this what you mean?" Then restate what the speaker said. Definitely avoid reflecting any feelings the interviewer expresses—for example, "You must be really frustrated by that," "Wow, how annoying," or "You sound really excited." Most interviewers would consider that type of communication to be odd.

The benefits of getting clarification are that it:

➤ Gives interviewers a well-articulated version of what they said and meant, which they generally appreciate hearing

➤ Gives the interviewer an "instant replay," so he or she can clarify a point, if needed

➤ Offers you the opportunity to confirm what you thought you heard

➤ Tells the interviewer you are listening

➤ Communicates respect to the interviewer

➤ Builds a connection

EXPRESSING YOURSELF EFFECTIVELY

Reflective communication is a flexible four-step process that's as much a mind-set as a strategy. For example, balance this approach with giving information about yourself and your ideas to advance your chances of getting the great job you want. Here are six tips:

LEARN ABOUT THE INTERVIEWER'S INTERESTS. Ask a few questions that show your interest in personal information the interviewer shares, such as winning a golf tournament. You can also strike up small talk by exercising your observation skills. Look for pictures on the wall or objects that suggest the interviewer's interests. *Briefly* mention a personal interest of yours, such as collecting wooden soldiers, golfing, or writing children's stories. This sharing approach can reduce tension and build rapport. However, be prepared to get down to the business of qualifying yourself for the job.

SHOW INTEREST IN THE ORGANIZATION. An interviewer may ask you what you know about the company. Your knowledge of the company's history and its current challenges is a factor within your control. If you do your homework on the company, you'll present as a knowledgeable job candidate. (Neglecting this area may raise doubts about your interest in the company.)

CREATE AN ATTITUDE OF BELONGING. If it seems natural, use the word "we" in reference to your role in the company. Watch to see if the interviewer favors this familiarity. If so, you are now presenting as a potential member of the team.

AVOID NEGATIVES. Disparaging a former employer is an example of a negative. Talking in negatives can lead an interviewer to rate you based on your negative views, which normally include a negative emotional tone. People tend to pay more attention to emotion, when it's apparent, than to verbal content.

PRESENT IN A PERSONABLE, KNOWLEDGEABLE, ENGAGING, AND COMPETENT MANNER. You can create this image of yourself in your mind and then convey it in the interview. Doing so may even be easier than you think.

NOTE WHERE YOU FIT INTO THE ORGANIZATION'S CULTURE. Blend your qualifications, motivation, energy level, and dedication into the conversation in a way that fits naturally.

To maintain a positive momentum in your reflective communications, periodically reflect internally on the process:

➢ Am I addressing the issues the interviewer wants to focus on?

➢ Am I linking my qualifications and experience to these issues?

➢ Is the interviewer responding favorably?

➢ Am I periodically checking with the interviewer to ensure that my answers fit the questions?

THE ART OF QUESTIONING

Asking questions is a basic part of communication. Questions can be closed ended or open ended.

Closed-ended questions evoke specific answers—for example, "What's the salary range for this position?" They frequently elicit a brief yes-or-no response, such as "Did you work for any other employer between 2009 and 2010?"

Phrases that signal closed-ended questions include "Are you…?" "Can you…?" and "Did you…?" This form of question discourages elaborate answers. Just because you're asked closed-ended questions doesn't mean you are locked into giving closed-ended answers, however. You can use closed-ended questions to add information by clarifying and qualifying: "I'd like to add…"

If the interviewer is interested only in asking closed-ended questions, you might have little chance to expand on issues. The interviewer may have a list of candidates scheduled and may get impatient if you appear to take too much time responding. However, you can turn this situation to your advantage. Use your own closed-ended question to clarify time limits: "So that I stay within the time you've allocated for the interview, how much time do we have?" That clarifying question can leave the interviewer with a positive impression. The answer can help you decide how to pace yourself in the interview.

You may have a few closed-ended questions. Here are some examples:

➢ *How soon do you want to fill this position?*

> ➤ *Can you tell me what is the required experience for the position?*

> ➤ *Is this a supervisory-level position?*

> ➤ *When can I expect to hear about your selection for this position?*

Open-ended questions offer latitude to expand, expound, and share ideas. They're a way for the interviewer to explore how you think and feel. Such questions include "Please describe…" "Tell me about…" "How…?" and "What…?"

Interviewers tend to use this open-ended format to get a better read on a candidate. However, as much as possible, keep your responses relevant to the job. For example, if your interviewer said, "Tell me how your family might react if you were on the road a week out of every month," an appropriate response might be that your family has adapted well to your current traveling schedule, which includes.…

You can use "what" and "how" questions to get clarification about the job and to gather useful information. "What" questions classify or define something—for example, "What do you mean when you say you are confident that some positions will soon open?"

"How" questions are useful for defining processes but also for identifying differences and similarities in situations: "How do my credentials compare with other candidates you have interviewed?" But "how" questions can put an interviewer on the spot. Your knowledge of the interviewer can temper this situation.

Do you know enough about your potential role in an organization to assess whether you'll fit into the organization well, and whether the role fits your short- and long-term career plans? When in doubt, ask questions to gain clarity.

PRACTICE, PRACTICE, PRACTICE

Mock interviews help you identify your strengths and what areas to correct as you build your confidence. We suggest finding a helpful and knowledgeable friend to act as the interviewer and record a video of several practice interviews. This extra step can help you identify the areas you want to develop and any habits that could distract an interviewer. Mock interviews give both visual and auditory feedback, better enabling you to pick up on consistent errors and fix them. If you notice yourself using distracting gestures or stock phrases (such as "you know"), be mindful of eliminating them. You can also pick up on other consistent but correctable errors, such as throat clearing or too many instances of "uh." Apologizing is also rarely helpful during an interview. The video can show you aspects of your posture; a tendency to slouch may not resonate well with an interviewer. Using video feedback also helps you notice what you do well so you can make a point of repeating those actions. If you come across as authentic and natural, that's a plus.

Reversing roles can add to your knowledge of how to interact with an interviewer. Do a mock interview with a friend where this time *you* play the interviewer. Looking at the process from this angle gives you additional insight into the process and how to present your qualifications.

STRATEGIES FOR SUCCESS

Communicating clearly can help you sell your ideas and competencies to an interviewer and gain that person's confidence that you can do the job.

KEY IDEAS

1.

2.

3.

ACTION STEPS

1.

2.

3.

IMPLEMENTATION

1.

2.

3.

RESULTS

1.

2.

3.

POSTSCRIPT

You can use reflective communication to gather information and shape your expressions for maximum positive impact in a job interview. In communicating with a possible employer, reflective communication can help you to think on your feet as you clearly express yourself. Applied well, reflective communication can break a tie in your favor. But you still have to sell your qualifications to boost your odds of getting the job you want.

9 MAKE THE MOST OF AN INTERVIEW OPPORTUNITY

You have researched an organization and matched the job functions from the job description against what you prefer to do, and you believe there's a good fit. The quality and content of your résumé helped an employer decide that you have the right education and work experience for the job, you've been invited for an interview, and you're prepared to make an ongoing positive impression. Still, you have to be on your toes.

When you are invited to a job interview, you know that the job pool has narrowed. Your next challenge is to help the hiring authority decide that you are the best candidate for the job.

Interviewing is a numbers game. The more interview experience you have, the more likely you'll develop an understanding of different interviewing styles and use this knowledge to bring about a favorable result. We'll help you address whatever apprehension you may have about interviewing, as well as share various issues an employer may raise in the interview. Preparing yourself this way can help you enter interview situations with greater confidence that you can advance the argument that you are the best candidate for the job. Moreover, the preparatory work

QUICK TIPS

➤ Developing a rapport with your interviewer may be more important than impressing the person with your skills.

➤ Have your ideas about the company, the job, and your qualifications organized in your mind so you can respond to questions spontaneously.

➤ Most interviewers will begin with small talk. Follow the lead until the interviewer signals it's time to get down to business.

➤ Whenever possible, respond in a positive way.

➤ Allow the interviewer to have the last word.

➤ Leave on a positive note.

you've done up to this point gives you a great foundation in self-efficacy to help you convey confidence.

PREPARE YOURSELF FOR THE INTERVIEW

Your first task is to prepare yourself emotionally for the interview. You want to be motivated to do your best while feeling relaxed, which is where you can apply the information from chapter 3 on pursuing your passion and optimizing your performance.

There's a maxim that people will remember how you made them feel long after they've forgotten what you said (attributed to Maya Angelou). The more relaxed you are, the more pleasant and affable you are likely to be. Here are three additional tips:

THIS IS NOT LIFE OR DEATH. As much as you may want this job, you don't absolutely *have* to get it. Other work opportunities are indeed out there for you, and sooner or later you will succeed at landing a good job. With this attitude, you will likely feel less pressured and be able to present in a relaxed manner.

AVOID PERFECTIONISTIC THINKING. Most likely you're not a professional entertainer, motivational speaker, or politician. It's unlikely you will be perfect in this situation or expected to be perfect. Just be yourself and follow the tips we describe, and you'll do fine.

KEEP PERSPECTIVE. Of course, you want to do well in this interview, but how well you do doesn't define you as a person. Your worth as a person is broader than an interview performance, even an excellent one. Have fun and do your best.

Three Interview Pitfalls

Following are three common interview pitfalls, each of which takes a good idea too far—preparing yourself and then overdoing it:

USING A CANNED PRESENTATION. You give a speech, describing your history and explaining why you believe you are right for the job. The advantage of this approach is that you can view yourself as controlling the agenda and expressing everything you want to say. The danger is that you may sound like a lecturer or a talking parrot. Canned sales presentations can do more harm than good with sophisticated interviewers. Perhaps a better approach would be to have some possible talking points outlined, to pull out as needed as the interview progresses.

GETTING PERSONAL AND ACTING AS IF THE INTERVIEWER IS AN OLD FRIEND. Picturing an interviewer in a positive way can lead to a positive attitude, but if you act overly familiar, there's no telling how the person will react. The interviewer may feel uncomfortable and view you as intrusive. Be friendly, but keep in mind that this is a formal business relationship.

ASSUMING THAT YOUR TALENTS ARE OBVIOUS, SO YOU SHOULD GET THE JOB. If you believe you are a great worker—whether you're a salesperson, manager, clerk, engineer, or quality-control specialist—you may assume that the interviewer *should* recognize your talents. Interviewers don't have ESP (extrasensory perception) and can't instinctively or intuitively fathom the depths of your skills. Your job is to sell the interviewer on your abilities without being pushy or trying too hard.

PRESENT YOURSELF PERSONABLY

Although describing your background and competency is certainly important, your interpersonal skills count more than giving the ideal answer to every question. People are first impressed by whether you care about them and their organization. Show interest and reasoned enthusiasm.

If you present in a friendly manner, on average, you will fare better than competitors who show little friendliness or curiosity about the organization. Interviewers prefer interviewees who approve of them. You can signal approval through a casual compliment that relates to one of the interviewer's strengths, something the person would agree with—for example, "I feel comfortable talking to you," "You ask very good questions," or "I appreciate that style because I, too, like to get to the heart of the matter." But sometimes there's a fine line between complimenting to express appreciation and complimenting to patronize. Be careful not to go overboard.

Interviewers are normally more impressed if your responses are honest, positive, and credible, so maintain a posture of friendly cordiality by commenting truthfully and positively about the work environment.

EXPLAIN WHY YOU SEEK EMPLOYMENT

If you are unemployed, the interviewer probably already knows this, and your employment status didn't disqualify you from advancing to the interview stage. Nevertheless, this issue is likely to come up.

Do you raise the issue or wait to see if the interviewer does? Unfortunately, there are no hard and fast rules. Preferably, you can dispense with the question at the beginning of a discussion, giving you more time to help the interviewer see how you'd be a big asset for the organization.

A credible reason typically resonates best: "As you may have heard, my company relocated to South Carolina, and my boss asked me to relocate. However, I have two teenagers in high school, making it a bad time to relocate. I enjoyed my job and coworkers, but the timing just wasn't right. I wanted to support my family in this area, and I felt confident I would find another good opportunity. That's why I'm here today."

As you think through your response, consider the employer's viewpoint. What can you say to put the matter into perspective for the interviewer and ease that person's mind, conveying that you are a credible candidate? Conversely, what can raise red flags? The following guidelines suggest how to address this sensitive topic:

> *Keep your explanation brief, concrete, and factual.* "Management downsized my area because of new, automated procedures and a downtrend in sales. The decision was based on seniority, so I and the three other newest team members were let go."

> *Avoid generalities.* Abstractions like "Things were going poorly, and I was let go" can invite more questions than you may want to answer.

> *Express yourself in a positive tone.* The confidence, consistency, and credibility in your statements send a constructive message. Interviewers may pay more attention to a "natural manner" and positive attitude than the general content.

PREPARE YOUR RESPONSES

Although a job search is a numbers game, your preparation for an interview is like playing golf with a pro as your partner. You gain an advantage toward getting your desired result.

When you meet a prospective employer, that person is as eager to fill the job as you are to work for the organization. Viewing this as a collaborative effort and doing your part sets a positive tone for the interview. In this process, you can count on answering questions designed to let the interviewer learn more about you and what you can do. Some interviewers have stock-in-trade questions such as, "Where do you see yourself in this organization five years from now?" Some carry out an interview in a more or less free-flowing style. Some do most of the talking. Since you can't anticipate every interviewer's style and questions, what can you do to influence the outcome?

You can prepare responses to common questions to show that you've done your homework and that you are a worthy competitor for the position. We'll start with seven sample questions and give examples of background research for answering them, as well as sample answers.

WHAT IS IT ABOUT OUR COMPANY THAT APPEALS TO YOU?

Research: Draw from information about the company you've read in the newspapers, the company's annual report, *The Value Line Investment Survey,* and Standard and Poor's and other business references, as well as what you learned through discussions with the organization's former and current employees. *Sample response:* "I know your company has a great reputation for quality. *Consumer Reports* rated your Speed Blender as a best buy and said it was virtually indestructible. I want to be part of an organization that strives for that level of excellence."

WHAT CAN YOU BRING TO OUR ORGANIZATION THAT OTHER CANDIDATES CAN'T?

Research: Focus on your accomplishments and explain how you can apply the same skills to produce quality results for that organization. Also, many companies now appreciate that character counts as much as skillfulness, so emphasizing traits like perseverance, work ethic, loyalty, and teamwork can go a long way. *Sample response:* "I have a strong work ethic and consistently complete my work well before deadlines." Concrete examples ordinarily have more impact than glittering generalities. Giving examples of times you worked in the evenings and weekends to meet an important deadline, why it was important to do, and what you accomplished may provide a positive impact.

WHAT ARE YOUR GREATEST LIMITATIONS?

Research: Draw on situations where you learned a different way based on a corrective experience. A common response is to turn a limitation into an asset. *Sample response:* Give a personal example where you took a corrective action—for example, "Once I set back an operation because I didn't give clear-enough directions. Since then I have made considerable progress at keeping people informed, and I keep working at doing better. I haven't heard any negative feedback on this issue in the past year."

WHAT DO YOU SEE YOURSELF DOING FIVE YEARS FROM NOW?

Research: Here, it can help to draw from your knowledge about the organization's people, products, processes, profits, promotions, and philosophy. Shaping your response to mesh with known opportunities in a company demonstrates that you see the organization as offering a career opportunity. (You can follow this question with a question, asking about expected opportunities within the organization so you have a frame of reference for your answer.) *Sample response:* "I intend to work hard and show my ability to effectively manage diverse problems. In the past five years, I have twice won the President's Cup for my sales accomplishments. I intend to improve on this performance. My goal now and over the next five years is to continually demonstrate that I merit taking additional responsibilities." (Applicants have been known to shoot themselves in the foot by telling the interviewer they would expect to have that person's job within five years.)

IF WE WERE TO REJECT YOUR APPLICATION, WHY DO YOU THINK WE'D DO SO? *Research:* What you know about the job description can come into play. Could the employer see you as being overqualified for the position? *Sample response:* If you think the question relates to overqualification, then consider answering with the unexpected—for example, "That's an interesting question. It likely wouldn't be because you didn't think I could do the job. It's unlikely that you would think I didn't have the experience to rise to the challenge of doing the job in an exemplary way. I know it wouldn't be because of my proven organization skills. It would likely be because you identified a candidate with higher-level experience." But if you make a response similar to this, be prepared to back up your statements with examples. If you think the question relates to underqualification, you can answer, "I am still in my first few years of employment and may appear less knowledgeable about widget production than candidates with many years of experience. On the other hand, I have spent the past five years learning new production methods and taking courses in technological advances in productivity enhancement, which I believe carry over into widget production."

WHAT SALARY ARE YOU LOOKING FOR? *Research:* Organizations normally publicize a salary range, but you can take an important step to prepare for such a question. Knowing the standard compensation for such a position in the industry and in the region will give you a frame of reference for responding reasonably. But you may also want to hedge. The organization already has an idea of what they'd offer. The following is one way to hedge. *Sample response:* "My salary is open to negotiation. When the time comes for us to discuss money, you will find that I'm realistic. I believe we can agree on a salary that meets our respective needs."

WHAT QUALIFIES YOU FOR THIS JOB? *Research:* Draw on your research about the company and the job. Knowing the job description and any problems management wants to solve can help you tie your qualifications to the job. *Sample response:* "I understand that KVM offers a unique financial management service to its customers and you want to expand the business. I enjoy contacting people and selling an idea I believe in. I believe in what you want to accomplish, and I would work hard to bring in new customers and to make KVM the top financial management consulting group in this region."

RESPOND EFFECTIVELY TO TOUGH QUESTIONS

Now it's your turn to think through potential responses to tough questions. Jot down your answers in a notebook or computer file, but be ready to make changes as you continue through this book. With experience and feedback, you might improve some of your responses.

1. Tell me about yourself.

    Research:

    Response:

2. What were your most noteworthy accomplishments in your last position?

    Research:

    Response:

3. Walk me through each item on your résumé (candidates who stumble over this type of question will likely have a short interview).

    Research:

Response:

4. What are three strengths and weaknesses of your last two supervisors?

   Research:

   Response:

5. What was your greatest accomplishment on your last job? How did you bring about that result?

   Research:

   Response:

6. What interests you the most (and least) about the position we have available?

   Research:

   Response:

7. Have you had to fire people? If so, describe the process you followed.

   Research:

   Response:

8. If we hired you, what actions would you take during your first six months with us? What results should we expect to see?

   Research:

   Response:

9. Tell me what you know about our products and customers.

   Research:

   Response:

10. How do you normally deal with deadline pressures?

    Research:

    Response:

11. Describe the people under your supervision whom you have helped develop, and tell me about their accomplishments.

    Research:

    Response:

12. Give me three examples of how you related to difficult supervisors.

    Research:

    Response:

13. How do you delegate authority?

    Research:

    Response:

14. Tell me what you learned from the last three books you read.

    Research:

    Response:

15. Would you be willing to relocate?

    Research:

    Response:

16. At the end of your career, what would you want people to say about your contributions?

    Research:

    Response:

17. If we hired you, do you think you could take over for your boss?

Research:

Response:

18. How would you respond to a demotion?

Research:

Response:

19. What rating and assessment did you receive in your last three performance reviews? May I look at those reviews?

Research:

Response:

INTERVIEW THE INTERVIEWER

Communication is a two-way street. It's important for you to decide whether an organization is a good place for you to work, and interviewing the interviewer can help you determine that. Whether you respond to an interviewer's invitation to ask questions or raise your own questions spontaneously, it's reasonable to ask the following:

➤ *Why are you hiring outside the organization for this position?*

➤ *If I were hired, what would be my reporting relationships?*

➤ *What would be my five most significant responsibilities?*

➤ *What opportunities does the organization provide for professional growth and advancement?*

➤ *Who are the people directly ahead of me on the organizational chart?* (You want to learn whether your promotional track is open or blocked.)

> ➤ *What new products or services are under consideration?*

> ➤ *What are the mission statement and guiding principles of the organization?*

> ➤ *What decisions would I be required to make?*

> ➤ *What are the most critical challenges the organization faces?*

> ➤ *What are the work attributes and personal qualities of people who are successful in the organization?*

This type of information can help you to decide whether this job is a reasonable choice for you. To help you prepare, next list the five most important questions for you to ask. For each, note why it's important to you to obtain this information.

IMPORTANT QUESTIONS TO ASK

Question 1:

Why it's important:

Question 2:

Why it's important:

Question 3:

Why it's important:

Question 4:

Why it's important:

Question 5:

Why it's important:

SPECIAL INTERVIEW SITUATIONS

You will likely encounter special, and even unexpected, interview situations, so it's in your best interest to be aware of and prepared for these. But avoid trying to cover all potential scenarios, which is impossible. Instead, develop a general approach that you feel comfortable adapting to changing situations.

CHANCE ENCOUNTERS: When you visit an organization, anyone you meet, including receptionists and other employees who speak to you, may be part of the interview process. The boss's administrative assistant may be especially influential. Without fawning, be unfailingly cordial.

THE TELEPHONE INTERVIEW: Interviewers may use telephone interviews when they feel pressed for time and have a pool of people to screen. Phone interviews present special challenges. Stick to the issues and tie your qualifications to the problems the interviewer presents for you to solve. Surplus information is unnecessary and may cause the interviewer to focus more on your uneasiness than your qualifications.

The telephone interviewer may assess how you articulate your thoughts, your tone of voice, the level of your qualifications, your interest in working for the company, and how well you field general questions. Making it through this phase will get you a face-to-face interview.

SKILL DEMONSTRATION: Employers tend to value people who can solve their problems. An interviewer may want to know if you can solve a pressing problem, clean up an embarrassing situation, or smooth over ruffled feathers, as well as what you would do to innovatively support the organization's mission. If skill demonstration doesn't come up and it seems appropriate, ask the interviewer to describe the types of problems you'd be expected to solve if you got the job. You are now in a position to talk about solving the problem.

Skill demonstration can help create a time investment on the part of an interviewer, making it less likely the person will want to drop you to pursue other candidates. Now that the interviewer has spent time listening to you, he or she will less likely want to spend the same amount of time with other candidates. Skill demonstrations can also help cause the interviewer to begin to see you as part of the team. Here are some additional tips:

> Ask to look at a copy of the job description, and ask what typical problems the company faces. This can lead to an open discussion about problem solving.

> Talk to department heads you would have contact with, and discuss their problems and how you could help.

> Ask to visit the work site. Observe and ask questions.

FOLLOW-UP INTERVIEWS

When an employer asks you back for a second interview, this is a sign of special interest. Before the meeting, pull together your information and notes, and review all you have learned about the company: what you have read, what people have said, and what you have seen. When feasible, find information about new strategies in the industry (that you didn't previously discuss during your interview) that relate to the company's production methods or services.

The second interview gives the decision maker an opportunity to get to know you in greater depth. You also get to know the organization and its people more fully. In the interview, focus on interacting. Do listen to the interviewer's long monologues. If you see this meeting turn to exploring a job offer, reemphasize your enthusiasm about the company and be specific about what you like about the company and the job opportunity. Speaking as if you were a part of the organization signals a positive attitude and sense of belonging.

Your interviewer may ask what you would do during the first few weeks of assuming your responsibilities. Here are a few ideas to consider:

> *I'd like to learn more about the company's people, products, and processes.*

> *I'd like to be exposed to the departments and people I'll be relating to.*

> *I'll look for ways to make my part of the operation more efficient and to support the procedures that work.*

> *I also appreciate the importance of the timing and pacing of change. I don't want to alter what's working well.*

> *I'll want to start making plans for changes in the areas upper management wants addressed first.*

> *I'll share my observations and insights, and I'll seek advice.*

STRATEGIES FOR SUCCESS

What did this chapter give you that you can apply to create opportunities for yourself through the interviewing process? To maximize the potential of reaching your goal, you might want to highlight what seems most useful to you.

KEY IDEAS

1.

2.

3.

ACTION STEPS

1.

2.

3.

IMPLEMENTATION

1.

2.

3.

RESULTS

1.

2.

3.

POSTSCRIPT

Interviews can be challenging, but they are also the prerequisite to a job opportunity. Thus, you have to take them seriously but not so seriously that you're uptight throughout the process.

In a tight job market, you may feel tempted to press harder to get a job, but consider an interviewer's perspective. This person may feel pressured by many candidates who are desperate for work. Presenting yourself personably, knowledgeably, and competently will likely separate you from the crowd. Your knowledge of the organization's past, products, processes, people, and prospects gives you an edge over candidates who see an opportunity for a job but haven't done their homework on the company. Look for opportunities to build what you know into your communication. As the proverb goes, "chance favors the prepared mind" (attributed to Louis Pasteur).

10 NEGOTIATE YOUR CONTRACT AND CLOSE THE DEAL

Now that you are in the final stretch, the time has come to negotiate an agreement and close the deal. Before you put on your dancing shoes, you need to prepare for this phase just as you have for other phases of your fearless job hunt.

You may not have the same luxury of representation in negotiating a work agreement as a professional athlete or an actor would, but this isn't ordinarily necessary.

Your discussions may be straightforward and uncomplicated, but, regardless, this is as critical a phase in your job search as any other. We take the position that it's better to be slightly overprepared than to go into a negotiation discussion underprepared. Unless you are in an exceptional position, the people you negotiate with are likely to be higher on the experience curve in this area. We'll help take some of the ambiguity out of this process.

Negotiable issues vary by the type and level of the position and by your negotiation leverage. Most complex negotiations are for higher-level specialty positions, such as higher management and in-demand specializations or professions. In the following section, we'll emphasize these complex areas, but if you are negotiating for an entry-level position, we think you'll find that many of the following issues apply, such as negotiating your salary.

WHAT'S YOUR LEVERAGE?

When negotiating with a company, both you and the organization have leverage. The organization has budgeted for the position and already knows its flexibility. You don't, and that awaits your discovery. Before deciding where you have leverage, consider the following:

> With a newly created position, there's often greater flexibility because management may not be certain what value to place on it.

> If your predecessor performed poorly, management may go the extra mile if they are convinced that you, as the replacement, have the skill and capability to prevent their previous problems from recurring. You may also be able to improve morale, which is worth a lot.

> If you bring a new skill set that will place the company in a more competitive position, with the likelihood of greater profitability, you have leverage.

> If the position lends itself to increased scope and function, and you declare your interest in expanding the responsibilities of the job, you have leverage.

QUICK TIPS

➤ Know your prospective employer by researching and gathering information on the company's compensation, benefits, and bonus packages.

➤ Regard the negotiation process as a problem-solving process.

➤ Find ways to resolve contentious issues.

➤ Regard an impasse as an opportunity for compromise.

➤ Reassure your prospective employer that you have a strong desire to be part of the company.

➤ Point out how your commitment and efforts can benefit the organization.

➤ Resist hesitating, second-guessing, and procrastinating about decision making.

➤ Work together with your prospective employer to produce a win-win situation.

➤ To support your side of the negotiations, back up your requests with good market research and background information on the industry.

NEGOTIATION IS AN ART AND A SCIENCE

You may know up front what your salary and benefits will be, or you may accept what you are first offered. But when there appears to be wiggle room on compensation and benefits, you have a negotiating opportunity.

Because both parties are presumably motivated to close the deal, and are looking for a fair and equitable resolution, the challenge is to find a way where both can win. The centerpiece of the deal is often the compensation package. As you enter the negotiation process, the key is to be well armed with relevant facts you can use to support your position.

Georgia describes her experience of entering the negotiation process:

> I made a point of spending hours in the library researching salaries, benefits, and bonus packages for account managers in the advertising field. I was well equipped to talk about trends in the advertising industry when I sat down to negotiate my employment arrangements. In my discussions with my potential employer, I made a point of gently introducing the data I had gathered. I didn't push the issues, but my future manager knew I had done my homework. He was most impressed, to say the least. Knowing I had done the research, he complimented me on my resourcefulness and offered me a competitive package. We were both pleased with the end results. Also, I told him to expect the same kind of resourcefulness when I started my new position with the company. My manager was excited to hear that. He wasn't disappointed.

TWO PSYCHOLOGICAL PITFALLS IN THE NEGOTIATION PROCESS

Jamie describes his negotiation process this way:

> I went into the meeting with the human resources manager and line manager thinking I had it made. I wasn't prepared for what followed. I just thought that if I was the one they wanted, I could call the shots. I figured I should get what I wanted because I was their best candidate. I was shocked to find they weren't prepared to offer me what I wanted. In fact, I almost lost the job. My future manager bluntly told me I was getting off on the wrong foot, that I should think about whether this was the right company for me. What an eye-opener!

From a human relations standpoint, setting demands is normally the wrong position to take. When you enter job negotiations with high expectations about what you think you're worth and then forcefully assert these expectations, you might put the other person on the defensive.

Rather than operate under assumptions, look at the initial phases of negotiations as exploratory and cooperative. The negotiating process is a give-and-take situation, where both parties would like to leave believing a fair deal was struck. The negotiations can shift into a cat-and-mouse game, where each party tries to figure out the other's limits.

Compensation is normally the key issue. But if you know the salary range the company operates with, as well as regional compensation standards for applicants with your education, experience, and talents, you are in a position to render reasoned judgments. Most employers are willing to make concessions, provided they are within budget for the position.

The Cost of Hesitation

Decision-making procrastination is needlessly postponing making a choice among your options or courses of action. You might typically delay making a decision under conditions of complexity and uncertainty, and when you underestimate your resources and capabilities. You may fear making a mistake, such as missing out on another opportunity.

Gillian describes her decision-making procrastination as follows:

The company offered me the job, but I waited and waited to see if there was something better out there for me. It was a weird reaction. I wanted a job badly, yet now that I had an offer, I wasn't sure it was good enough. The negotiations had gone well; I got most of what I was looking for, yet I didn't give them a firm commitment. They continued to ask me if anything was wrong and said they needed an answer. I kept putting them off. I hesitated because I had convinced myself that there was something better for me that I hadn't yet discovered. So, the employer eventually offered the job to someone else. In due time I got another position, but did I learn a lesson!

Map Your Expectations

As you prepare for the negotiation process, decide what's important, what's useful, and what you can afford to throw away. Before you enter the negotiation process, here are some questions to ponder to help crystallize what you hope to accomplish:

> ➤ What's most important to you?

> ➤ What starting salary do you want?

> ➤ How important is a good benefits package, and what if you can't secure your ideal package?

> ➤ What perks are you seeking, and what compromises are you prepared to make?

> ➤ What are the responsibilities for your new position, and are they consistent with what you expected?

> ➤ How important is a job description to you, and if one doesn't exist for the position, what do you plan to do?

> ➤ What type of reporting relationship do you prefer, and will that exist in your new position?

> ➤ How important is the job title to you, and are you satisfied with the title of the position?

> ➤ How much are you prepared to travel?

> ➤ What are you prepared to trade?

> ➤ What do you consider to be nonnegotiable?

Prep Yourself for Action

Preparing for your negotiation process includes determining what you'll minimally accept and would ideally like to have. Making a reasoned judgment involves at least two questions: what do you know about the company and the position, and what can you control? So, if possible, get the following questions answered:

- ➤ *Job title:* Is it fixed, or can it be modified?

- ➤ *Job responsibilities:* Is there the option to assume more responsibilities down the road for additional compensation?

- ➤ *Job description:* Can it be modified, depending on my performance?

- ➤ *Salary range for the position:* Where in the salary range will I be placed, and will my experience influence that placement?

- ➤ *Benefits package:* Is the benefits plan a comprehensive one, or is it a menu-driven plan?

- ➤ *Amount of travel required for the position:* What does the organization cover during company travel?

- ➤ *Vacation entitlement:* How will my previous experience impact the number of weeks I receive?

- ➤ *Reporting relationship:* How many people will I report to, and how will that influence my performance review?

- ➤ *Perks:* Are these perks performance based?

- ➤ *Bonus structure:* Is it performance based or based on the profit and loss of the company as a whole?

- ➤ *Salary review period:* What period of time needs to pass before a review—for example, three months or six months—and can it be shortened?

- ➤ *Signing bonus:* When do I receive the bonus, upon signing or once I start work?

If you want the job, be careful how tenacious you are in pursuing these and any other questions you have. Pay attention to how the employer reacts, and prepare to adjust your responses to the situation you observe.

IDENTIFY NEGOTIABLE ISSUES

Now that you are prepared to negotiate and discuss matters important to both you and your prospective employer, there's a list of negotiable matters to keep in mind. With each negotiable item is a list of suggestions to help you get the best possible offer.

We cover a broad range of negotiable issues, so you may find that some are inapplicable, but use what applies to your situation.

Salary

The most noteworthy item for negotiation is your salary.

> ➤ Aim for the highest salary you can possibly obtain.

> ➤ Avoid committing to a specific salary until you receive a concrete offer.

> ➤ If you are given a salary offer, that's likely a starting point for negotiation.

> ➤ Most employers expect to receive a counteroffer.

> ➤ Use your industry data and company information to strengthen your counteroffer.

> ➤ If the company presents a salary range during negotiations, respond that the range sounds interesting and that you are reasonable and flexible, then attempt to get your employer to commit to a specific figure that you can work from.

> ➤ Because of company policy for new hires, the employer may be firm in its salary offer and unwilling to create a precedent for a higher starting salary. In this case, look for other items to discuss, such as a company car, its make and model, personal use of the car, and other allowances.

> ➤ Discuss the number of functions you will perform, because some companies establish function-based salaries—that is, the more responsibilities, the higher the salary.

➤ If necessary, declare your prior salary as a reference point for negotiation. Indicate that you would prefer a little more because of the high-quality work you will deliver.

➤ Be certain to receive a guarantee that a potentially unsatisfactory profit-and-loss statement won't negatively impact your salary.

Signing Bonus

If a company can't meet your salary requirements, consider discussing a signing bonus.

➤ Once again, use your industry data and company information to solidify your request.

➤ Determine when this bonus will be paid.

➤ Request a review of your salary status at six months and again after one year.

➤ Pin down the exact salary increase you will receive after each review if you meet or exceed performance expectations.

➤ Be sure to have this arrangement written into your letter of agreement with your new employer.

Benefits

Next to salary, the benefits package is the most important item for negotiation.

➤ Establish with your prospective employer the range of coverage in the benefits plan.

➤ Determine the extent of medical coverage available through the plan.

➤ Ascertain the extent of dental coverage obtainable through the plan.

> ➤ Establish whether the company insures itself or employs an outside firm to provide the insurance. This will affect the range of coverage available to you.

> ➤ Determine the medical coverage options open to you should you experience a catastrophic illness or accident.

> ➤ Certain companies provide different levels of coverage. Should you require enhanced coverage, ascertain whether your prospective employer will permit you to upgrade.

Start Date and Vacation Entitlement

If you sense urgency in the employer for you to start as soon as possible, you might think twice about discussing your planned vacation and asking to take time off before starting. You can note these plans and show a willingness to forego them, which shows a willingness to accommodate and to step up and start contributing right away.

> ➤ Determine when the employer wants you to start.

> ➤ Declare when you are available to start.

> ➤ If there's a big discrepancy between the company's preferences and yours, it might be wise to defer to your employer's wishes.

> ➤ This is also a useful opportunity to negotiate your vacation entitlement. Armed with industry standards, previous vacation arrangements, and current company policy, present the number of weeks you would want as your vacation entitlement.

> ➤ Determine whether the weeks of vacation entitlement can be divided and taken throughout the year. Some companies prefer that an employee take all due vacation time at once.

> ➤ Discuss the possibility of carrying over vacation time to the next year. Many companies prefer that the vacation allotment

be used only during the calendar year. If you don't take the time during the calendar year, you may lose it.

Relocation Costs

Relocation costs include a variety of expenses involved in moving from your current location to another one. Often, the cost of changing jobs can be high.

➤ Determine whether your employer will provide you with a real estate agent to help you and your family locate a new house.

➤ Ascertain whether your employer will provide a school consultant to help you locate the best possible school for your children.

➤ Check whether your company will pick up the costs associated with using consultants.

➤ Determine whether your company will pay the furniture- and auto-moving costs.

➤ If you are moving to a location with a higher cost of living, determine whether your company will provide a financial subsidy.

➤ Relocation may involve moving from an area with lower real estate costs and lower mortgage payments to an area with higher real estate costs and higher mortgage payments. Check whether the company will cover the difference in mortgage payments.

➤ If not, determine whether the company will give you a low-interest-bearing or non-interest-bearing loan to cover the difference, the repayment of which can come out of your salary over time.

➤ In some instances a house might not sell so quickly. Determine whether your prospective employer will assume the responsibility for the sale of your home if it doesn't sell within a reasonable period—say, six months.

➤ Ascertain whether your company will provide a bridge loan to purchase a new house until your former residence is sold.

➤ Because some relocations involve considerable added expenses, establish whether the company will provide you with a bonus to cover your extraordinary relocation costs.

Travel Expenses

Regular travel can be disruptive and draining at times. Determine whether your company will provide airline club privileges, a company jet, and so on, making it easier for you to board, fly, and disembark. Traveling will then be more comfortable and convenient.

Club Memberships

In certain jobs—namely, high-visibility positions in sales, marketing, or business development—club memberships are important as an avenue for developing business leads, securing new business, and rewarding existing clients. If you are negotiating for this type of position:

➤ Establish whether your company will support club memberships.

➤ Determine the number of memberships your company will pay for.

➤ Ascertain whether your company will cover all the membership costs, will provide partial costs, or would prefer sharing the costs with you.

➤ Determine whether your company will pay your registration fee in a fitness club. Because of the current emphasis on employee wellness, many organizations encourage their employees to enroll in fitness clubs by paying all the costs or sharing the costs.

Stock Options

In an effort to attract and retain valued employees, some companies offer stock options.

➤ Determine when the stock options kick in.

➤ Ascertain the number of stocks the company is prepared to offer you and their base value.

➤ Establish how long you are required to hold these options before you can cash them in.

Contributory Pension Plans and Savings Plans

Companies offer pension and savings plans as another way to attract and retain employees.

➤ Determine whether the plans are contributory or noncontributory. Noncontributory plans are those where the company is the sole contributor.

➤ Ascertain how long until you are vested. (Often you have to be an employee with the company for a specific number of years before you can access the plans, especially if they are noncontributory.)

➤ If the plans are contributory, meaning you contribute as well as the company, establish whether you can increase your participation and whether the company will match that increase.

TO RENEGOTIATE OR NOT

Now that you have completed negotiations and the process has provided a win-win situation for both you and your prospective employer, it might be wise to reflect on what decisions were made and whether you are truly comfortable with the results. If you aren't comfortable, it would be unwise to sign the employment agreement, and signing despite your reservations would likely negatively affect your performance. So, as you contemplate what was decided, ask yourself the following questions and think of any others you might have:

- ➤ Upon reexamination, does the total package agreed upon meet my needs?

- ➤ Is the salary commensurate with my responsibilities?

- ➤ How did family and close friends react to the package I negotiated?

- ➤ Have any conditions changed for me?

- ➤ If the job requires relocation, how easy will it be for my spouse or partner to obtain a position in a new region, if desired? Are the living conditions and schools in the new region suitable?

- ➤ Is the medical and dental coverage sufficient for me and my family?

Unless there are extraordinary reasons for you not to sign on, proceed with the negotiated agreement. To attempt to renegotiate at this point would likely seriously jeopardize your position with the company, and the employer could possibly withdraw the offer.

SEARCH FIRMS

If you used a search firm, the offer to hire will pass from the company to the firm to you. The firm is the intermediary, although the company will often inform you of their intention to proceed with an offer.

As the go-between, the search firm will handle the negotiations between you and your prospective employer. Search firms on retainer will already have prepared the package in advance and often know what to expect with any upcoming negotiations. However, search firms want to close the deal, because they serve not only the company's interests but also your interests, especially if the company wants you on their team. The search firm acts like a real estate broker, serving the interests of both the vendor and the buyer.

STRATEGIES FOR SUCCESS

Now that you have completed this chapter, it's important to not only reflect on what you've read but also record key points that will allow you to push forward. The negotiation process is, in essence, the final activity in your job hunt, but it's a very vital one, so it's still crucial to remain focused and motivated and to actively plan your concluding steps in finally fulfilling your goal of landing a great position.

KEY IDEAS

1.

2.

3.

ACTION STEPS

1.

2.

3.

IMPLEMENTATION

1.

2.

3.

RESULTS

1.

2.

3.

POSTSCRIPT

After the search is over and you have secured your dream job—or, if not your dream job, at least a meaningful position—it's time to celebrate! Pat yourself on the back for your commitment and determination, and rest assured these same characteristics will stand you in good stead in the job you are about to start.

SUGGESTED READING

Bolles, R. N. 2009. *What Color Is Your Parachute?* Berkeley, CA: Ten Speed Press.

Dawson, K. M., and S. N. Dawson. 2008. *Job Search: The Total System—Achieve Your Better Job, Better Pay, Better Life!* 3rd ed. Houston, TX: Total Career Resources.

Ellis, A. 2003. *Ask Albert Ellis: Straight Answers and Sound Advice from America's Best-Known Psychologist.* Atascadero, CA: Impact Publishers.

———. 2006. *How to Stubbornly Refuse to Make Yourself Miserable About Anything: Yes, Anything!* New York: Citadel Press Books.

Ellis, A., and R. A. Harper. 1997. *A Guide to Rational Living.* 3rd ed. Chatsworth, CA: Wilshire Book Company.

Klarreich, S. 2008. *Pressure-Proofing: How to Increase Personal Effectiveness on the Job and Anywhere Else for That Matter.* New York: Routledge.

Knaus, W. J. 1982. *How to Get Out of a Rut.* Englewood Cliffs, NJ: Prentice-Hall.

———. 2002. *The Procrastination Workbook: Your Personalized Program for Breaking Free from the Patterns That Hold You Back.* Oakland, CA: New Harbinger Publications.

———. 2008. *The Cognitive Behavioral Workbook for Anxiety: A Step-by-Step Program.* Oakland, CA: New Harbinger Publications.

———. In press. *End Procrastination Now! Get It Done with a Proven Psychological Approach.* New York: McGraw-Hill.

Pierson, O. 2006. *The Unwritten Rules of the Highly Effective Job Search: The Proven Program Used by the World's Leading Career Services Company.* New York: McGraw-Hill.

REFERENCES

Atkinson, W. 2004. Stress: Risk management's most serious challenge? *Risk Management* 51 (6):20–24.

Bandura, A. 1997. *Self-Efficacy: The Exercise of Control*. New York: W. H. Freeman and Company.

Beck, B. L., S. R. Koons, and D. L. Milgrim. 2000. Correlates and consequences of behavioral procrastination: The effects of academic procrastination, self-consciousness, self-esteem, and self-handicapping. *Journal of Social Behavior and Personality* 15 (5):3–13.

Birdwhistell, R. L. 1970. *Kinesics and Context: Essays on Body Motion Communication*. Philadelphia: University of Pennsylvania Press.

Blascovich, J. 2008. Challenge and threat. In *Handbook of Approach and Avoidance Motivation*, ed. A. J. Elliot, 431–44. New York: Psychology Press.

Brown, L. E. 2008. Job seekers on the Internet: An empirical analysis. *Humanities and Social Sciences* 69 (4A):1562.

Cooley, C. H. 1902. *Human Nature and the Social Order*. New York: Charles Scribner's Sons.

Covey, S. R. 1989. *The 7 Habits of Highly Effective People: Powerful Lessons in Personal Change*. New York: Simon and Schuster.

David, D., A. Szentagotai, K. Eva, and B. Macavei. 2005. A synopsis of rational-emotive behavior therapy (REBT): Fundamental and applied research. *Journal of Rational-Emotive and Cognitive-Behavior Therapy* 23 (3):175–221.

Della-Posta, C., and P. D. Drummond. 2006. Cognitive behavioural therapy increases re-employment of job seeking worker's compensation clients. *Journal of Occupational Rehabilitation* 16 (2):223–30.

Ellis, A. 2003. *Ask Albert Ellis: Straight Answers and Sound Advice from America's Best-Known Psychologist.* Atascadero, CA: Impact Publishers.

Ellis, A., and D. Ellis. In press. *Rational Emotive Behavior Therapy Monograph: APA Theories of Psychology Series.* Washington, DC: American Psychological Association.

Epstude, K., and N. J. Roese. 2008. The functional theory of counterfactual thinking. *Personality and Social Psychology Review* 12 (2):168–92.

Fisher, A. 2001. Enjoy being unemployed? Keep job hunting online. *Fortune*, January 22, 143.

Franklin, B. 1986. *Benjamin Franklin: The Autobiography and Other Writings.* Ed. Kenneth Silverman. New York: Penguin.

Freud, S. 1947. *The Ego and the Id.* 4th ed. Trans. Joan Riviere. London: Hogarth Press.

Ganley, A. L., and G. S. Elias. 1966. *Know Yourself.* New York: McGraw-Hill.

Hodgins, D. C., L. E. Ching, and J. McEwen. 2009. Strength of commitment language in motivational interviewing and gambling outcomes. *Psychology of Addictive Behaviors* 23 (1):122–30.

Holland, J. L. 1996. Exploring careers with a typology: What we have learned and some new directions. *American Psychologist* 51 (4):397–406.

Kahneman, D., A. B. Krueger, D. Schkade, N. Schwarz, and A. A. Stoneger. 2006. Would you be happier if you were richer? A focusing illusion.

Princeton University Center for Economic Policy Studies (CEPS) working paper no. 125.

Kanfer, R., C. R. Wanberg, and T. M. Kantrowitz. 2001. Job search and employment: A personality-motivational analysis and meta-analytic review. *Journal of Applied Psychology* 86 (5):837–55.

Kelly, W. 1972. *Pogo: We Have Met the Enemy and He Is Us*. Riverside, NJ: Simon and Schuster.

Klassen, R. M., L. L. Krawchuk, and S. Rajani. 2008. Academic procrastination of undergraduates: Low self-efficacy to self-regulate predicts higher levels of procrastination. *Contemporary Educational Psychology* 33 (4):915–31.

Knaus, W. J. 1983. *How to Conquer Your Frustrations*. www.rebtnetwork. org/library/How_to_Conquer_Your_Frustrations.pdf.

———. 2006. *The Cognitive Behavioral Workbook for Depression*. Oakland, CA: New Harbinger Publications.

———. In press. *End Procrastination Now! Get It Done with a Proven Psychological Approach*. New York: McGraw-Hill.

McCrea, S. M. 2008. Self-handicapping, excuse making, and counterfactual thinking: Consequences for self-esteem and future motivation. *Journal of Personality and Social Psychology* 95 (2):274–92.

McCrea, S. M., N. Liberman, Y. Trope, and S. J. Sherman. 2008. Construal level and procrastination. *Psychological Science* 19 (12):1308–14.

McEwen, B., and E. Lasley. 2007. Allostatic load: When protection gives way to damage. In *The Praeger Handbook on Stress and Coping*, vol. 1, ed. A. Monat, R. S. Lazarus, and G. Reevy, 99–109. Westport, CT: Praeger/Greenwood Publishing Group.

Morin, W. J., and L. Yorkes, 1982. *Outplacement Techniques: A Positive Approach to Terminating Employees*. New York: Drake Beam Morin.

Richardson, K. M., and H. R. Rothstein. 2008. Effects of occupational stress management intervention programs: A meta-analysis. *Journal of Occupational Health Psychology* 13 (1):69–93.

Rogers, C. R. 1961. *On Becoming a Person: A Therapist's View of Psychotherapy.* Boston, MA: Houghton Mifflin.

Sirois, F. M. 2004. Procrastination and counterfactual thinking: Avoiding what might have been. *British Journal of Social Psychology* 43 (pt. 2):269–86.

Terkel, L. "Studs." 1972. *Working.* New York: Pantheon.

Thoresen, C. J., S. A. Kaplan, A. P. Barsky, C. R. Warren, and K. de Chermont. 2003. The affective underpinnings of job perceptions and attitudes: A meta-analytic review and integration. *Psychological Bulletin* 129 (6):914–45.

Toth, C. 1993. Effect of résumé format on applicant selection for job interviews. *Applied H. R. M. Research* 4 (2):115–12.

Tracey, T. J. G. 2008. Adherence to RIASEC structure as a key career decision construct. *Journal of Counseling Psychology* 55 (2):146–57.

Tracey, T. J. G., and S. B. Robbins. 2006. The interest-major congruence and college success relation: A longitudinal study. *Journal of Vocational Behavior* 69 (1):64–89.

Tsabari, O., A. Tziner, and E. I. Meir. 2005. Updated meta-analysis on the relationship between congruence and satisfaction. *Journal of Career Assessment* 13 (2):216–32.

U.S. Department of Labor. 1991. *Dictionary of Occupational Titles.* 4th ed., rev. Washington, DC: U.S. Department of Labor, Employment and Training Administration, U.S. Employment Service.

———. In press. *The Occupational Outlook Handbook, 2010–2011: With Bonus Content.* Bureau of Labor Statistics. St. Paul, MN: Jist Works.

U.S. Equal Employment Opportunity Commission and U.S. Department of Justice. 1991. *Americans with Disabilities Act Handbook.* 1991. Washington, DC: U.S. Equal Employment Opportunity Commission and U.S. Department of Justice.

van Eerde, W. 2003. A meta-analytically derived nomological network of procrastination. *Personality and Individual Differences* 35 (6):1401–18.

von Clausewitz, C. 1968. *On War.* New York: Penguin.

Wanberg, C. R., T. M. Glomb, Z. Song, and S. Sorenson. 2005. Job-search persistence during unemployment: A 10-wave longitudinal study. *Journal of Applied Psychology* 90 (3):411–30.

Wanberg, C. R., R. Kanfer, and J. T. Banas. 2000. Predictors and outcomes of networking intensity among unemployed job seekers. *Journal of Applied Psychology* 85 (4):491–503.

Bill Knaus, Ed.D., is a licensed psychologist in Massachusetts who was responsible for the development of a powerful personnel selection system that was associated with significant productivity gain. His specialties include the treatment of depression, anxiety, and substance abuse, frustration tolerance training, and overcoming procrastination. He has authored over twenty books, including five on overcoming procrastination.

Sam Klarreich, Ph.D., is president of The Berkeley Centre for Effectiveness in Toronto, Canada. He is author of *Pressure Proofing* and five other books.

Russell Grieger, Ph.D., is a licensed clinical psychologist in private practice and president of Russell Grieger and Associates, an organizational consulting company. An adjunct professor at the University of Virginia, Grieger has authored six books and over seventy-five professional papers and chapters.

Nancy Knaus, MBA, Ph.D., is director of psychological services at Monson Developmental Center. She has more than thirty years of experience working with people with intellectual disabilities and implementing rational emotive education. Responsible for hiring psychology staff, she employs sophisticated assessment center technologies.

Foreword writer **George S. Elias, Ed.D.,** has been actively involved in career guidance as an educator, counselor, and consultant to the Departments of Labor, Defense, Education, the U.S. Equal Employment Opportunity Commission (EEOC), and the National Council on Disability.

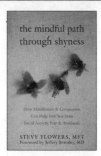

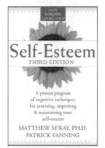